New Haven Ratchet Business

Business

Part 1

by

Stacey Fenner

40,000 words

ISBN 978-1539008910

CONTENTS

Visit Stacey Fenner's Facebook for the latest news and updates.

Instagram: authorstaceyfenner

Twitter: @sfenner1

Facebook: www.facebook.com/authorstaceyfenner

DEDICATION

In memory of my brother, Darin Fenner. I love you brother.

Lord knows I'm missing you, but your sister is still at it, doing what you would want me to do!

Gone but never forgotten. Always in my heart!

ACKNOWLEDGMENTS

I'd like to thank God for giving me this gift; I can't do anything without my Lord and Savior.

As always I have to thank my father and mother, Lester and Paulette, for everything they have done for me and still do!

To my wonderful husband, Keith, thank you for being my rock. I love you! To my two beautiful daughters, Jasmine & Janay, I love you more than life itself. Once again, thank you for your patience! To my Nook, you give me a run for my money, but G-Ma loves you! To my wonderful family, thank you all for all your support!

Too many to name, but thank you to my irky cousin, Safiya Staggers, for inspiring me to write this book!

To the team of people that help me on a daily basis in so many different ways; my everything, Gayle Wise, Mike, Shartarra, Erica, and my cousin, Anna Spruill. I thank each and every one of you!

Thank you to my newly found family, UUB. I thank each and every one of you!

Last, but not least, to all my readers. I couldn't do this without you. Thank you from the bottom of my heart!

CHAPTER 1

THE BUM SQUAD

I'm Poncho. I guess you could say I'm the ladies man out the squad. I'm the one with the swag to reel them in. I make a woman feel like she's God's greatest gift. When I'm with a woman I make her feel special. I was put here on earth to give any woman that I touch the attention that her body craves and yearns for. I'm that man that feels desires.

Women get addicted to me and chase me like I'm crack. I'm that drug that they can never get enough of, which is good for my ego, but it comes with problems.

I'm always getting caught up but I can't help myself. I don't have a preference. I just love all women. Shapes, sizes, colors...it don't matter. No woman is off limits to me. I don't care if she's married, in a relationship; she could be with my brother or one of my squad and I'll still tap that ass, or should I say, sweet spot. Yes, I will talk a woman right out of her panties.

Women take good care of me too…after I service them. My boys say I'm pimping them, but they're getting that long, deep stroke, a tongue bath, and a full body massage as an extra bonus. What also helps me is the fact that I could be a brother to Morris Chestnut. I'm just a fine piece of chocolate. What can I say…I was born this way.

*****

Growing up in a household full of women taught me a lot about a woman's mind. I have five sisters, and I watched each and every one of them play these dudes for a fool. My sisters broke a lot of hearts. They knew how to milk the hell out of a nigga and suck him dry. When they could no longer supply the need, it was bounce time. They had no use for them anymore.

The chicks that I dealt with always called themselves getting close to one of my sisters; I call it trying to buy a friendship because it was phony as fuck. I don't know why they thought that hanging with one of my sisters was going to get them some brownie points. Half the time my sisters were all hooked up in the plan to begin with. I would have one chick walking out and the other walking in.

My sisters were just as cruddy as me, so they weren't doing nothing but making it easier for me to do what I do best. Keep hanging with my sisters and running off at the mouth; I was always two steps ahead. When are females going to realize that blood is thicker than water, and the way I went through women, you weren't going to be around for long anyway.

*****

Liz was my main squeeze, everyone knew that, but chicks didn't care. Anyway they could have me was enough for them, until they fell all in love. When I saw that coming it was time to cut her off. But all things come to an end.

After ten years of dealing with the lies and my cheating ass, Liz put me the hell out and it looks like she ain't looking back. Liz was my high school sweetheart; she's the mother of three of my daughters, so I will always have much respect for her. She's the only one of my baby mama's that I'm cool with, besides Chris.

*****

I have eleven kids in total, with more to come; I'm sure of it. These women are always trying to tie me down with these babies. I love all my children, but dealing with eight baby mamas and their attitudes makes it hard for a dude like me. As soon as I don't do what they want me to, then I'm shit on a stick! My life is always filled with drama, I can't escape it.

*****

Now my right hand man, Rich, used to be heavy in the drug game, but once the feds got involved and niggas started getting a hundred years and shit, he got out quick. I don't blame him.

Freedom was everything to me. The streets lost a lot of respect for him once he got out the game. They considered him to be a sell-out and a bitch-ass.

I never understood how you could get mad at the next man because he doesn't want to go to jail. Rich had already been there a time or two, and from what he told me, he wasn't fond of that shit. If getting out of the game kept him on these streets rather than behind them bars, I was with that. He wasn't no snitch. Rich never ratted anybody out. He just made a rash decision to walk straight. I guess after he did that two-year stretch it must have opened his eyes up. Normally, he would go in and get right out, but not that last time; the judge made him sit for a while. When my man was gone I missed the hell out of him. I'm close to all my boys, but Rich is the one that I really ride for.

Now this fool decided to settle down and get married to Dominique. She is a good woman. The whole time Rich was away, Dominique held him down, and as far as know, she never strayed. If she did, it hasn't come out yet. Now that Rich don't have them dollars anymore she's been holding the family down.

During those two years that Rich was away, Dominique really got her shit together for her and them kids. She went to school for a PCA and landed a good job at Yale. She's been there ever since.

I guess you can say he hooked up with one of the good ones; that's about a little something in New Haven. She was down when he had money, and she stayed with him now that he has no money. Most women would have run away by now.

*****

That's why I let women know off the rip that I don't have anything to offer but some dick and conversation. All that providing mess just isn't me. They can't miss what I never did.

When things get rough and these women start requiring more of me, that's when it's time for me to bounce on up out of there. Then when I bounce they start acting a fool, wanting me back, acting all crazy! Women don't know what they want. They're all confused and shit.

*****

Right now, for the past couple of years, I've been living with Chris, one of my baby mamas. Things are cool now because I kind of do what I want to do, just in a respectful way.

She's been trained very well by me. Don't check my phone, never come looking for me, and don't look for shit that you know you aren't ready to handle. Please don't ask me a lot of questions that you know damn well you're not going to get the truth from. All I have is a bunch of lies. Whatever you want to hear is what I will tell you.

Once Chris got that down pat, things been rolling nice and smooth. Plus, she understands that I never plan on working, but I manage to keep a few dollars in my pocket and a fresh ride, even if it isn't mine.

*****

Quan is a real smooth dude. We were all raised up together on the hill on Howard Ave, until his mother bought a house in Westville. He still managed to make his way to us boys, for life is what we are.

Quan was the type that had everything handed to him as a child. His moms spoiled the hell out of her only child. Nigga always had money with the freshest gear, but when Moms passed, Quan went through that life insurance money like it was water. He had the house, but ended up losing it after he didn't pay the taxes on it. Rich paid them for him when he had money like that.

Now Quan's family was holding a grudge against him because they felt like he didn't do right by his mother. He lost everything that she worked so hard for. He was young and dumb. Twenty-two years old with thousands of dollars. He didn't know what to do with it back then.

*****

Shit, we had a different car for every day of the week, clubbing it up, and our choice in females. We lived for the weekend. On Friday nights we would bar hop, just walk through and make our presence be known, then bounce back out. On Saturday mornings we took a daily run to New York to get our outfits for the night, then on the way back we would stop at the Chapel Square Mall and hang out with the crowd until they closed. Then we would go back to Quan's house, shower and change to get ready to go to the club.

Whatever spot we chose is where Quan had a bad habit of buying out the bar. Normally we didn't arrive until midnight, but that hour and a half did some serious money damage.

Rich and I tried to tell him not to do it, but after a couple of drinks, nigga would lose his mind and do it anyway. When the money got low so did we. Not that we were hiding, we just weren't clubbing and barhopping anymore. Just ho hopping! Now women were our problems!

*****

Quan's been messing with Tisha, on an off, for the last five years. All of a sudden, he developed a preference in women, the bigger the better for him. That little chick broke his heart, and had him crying like a little bitch. He hadn't been like that since his moms passed away. He claims that has nothing to do with his preference, but me and the fellas know better than that.

That heartbreak took a toll on him. We didn't even see him; he disappeared for months trying to get himself together. I'm never going to have a woman get me like that, too much pussy out here for that.

Quan was messing with Tisha's best friend, Crystal, that's how he met her. I guess it all worked out in his favor because to this day that's still her best friend.

I need a woman in my life like that, one that believes in sharing. I told him he needs to be doing them both, since it's all cool and the gang. I know I would be. Let me find a hook up like that one...I'll be in heaven.

*****

My boy's, Trey and Mickey, they weren't like us. We call them the Mr. Moms of the crew. Chicks have them running around with their heads cut off. We see them when they're able to get a free pass. They have to pick up and drop off kids, clean the house, wash the clothes, babysit, cook; you name it. Anything other than working, they're doing it. If you ask me, they're better off just getting a job instead of doing all of that.

They look at me like I got it made when they could be having the same opportunities as me, but neither one of them wanted to leave the playground that they played in, which was Church Street South Projects. They had a reputation for running through them women, or sometimes going back and forth with the same ones. It was like playing musical chairs with a bunch of women. Then the women would get to fighting over them.

Some of the best fights I ever seen would be going down in the South. Hair flying, shirts being ripped off, legs all up in the air; me and the boys call it a strip fight!

As much as we tried to talk those two into leaving them project chicks alone, they wouldn't. When we're on our ho stroll just hollering at chicks, once she said she didn't live in the projects, it was a wrap for them.

Crazy how that was a turn off for them and a turn on for me. I need a woman with a good paying job. Somebody has to take care of me. A woman not doing anything with herself was of no use to me, and there was no future of ever being with me. Now don't get me wrong, I will fuck her, but she will never hit the relationship status with me. I don't want a bum ass bitch!

CHAPTER 2

KEISHA

"Hello," I answered the phone for my ride or die chick, Chris.

Everyone else's calls could wait. We might have lost contact when I got expelled from Wilbur Cross High School, but ever since I ran into her at the Freddy Fixer Parade we've been glued together like we were never apart.

"Hey Keisha, what are you doing?" Chris asked.

"I'm trying to flat iron this raggedy weave. My money is so tight I can't afford to buy no hair right now." *The first isn't getting here quick enough. I need my check.* "I'm getting ready to call Rich's wife and let her know that he's out here cheating on us."

"Girl what? Who's he messing with now?" Chris said it like this is something he does on a regular. *Hmmm, I wonder what she's not telling me.*

"Man Chris, Wanda called me last night. He was hugged up with some chick at Ballards. Wanda said they came in together and left together. She even sent me a picture of them toasting it up at the bar, so I have the evidence sitting right here in my phone. There is no getting out of this one." *I can't wait to see Rich. I got something for him.* "He will be dealt with; playing with me!" I said angrily.

"Girl, you know how they do us when we're pregnant. He done went and found him something to play with until you drop that load." Chris replied.

"Oh I'm going to play now. For six years I've been quiet and faithful. Here I am eight months pregnant, about to go in any day now, and you out having fun with the next chick. I'm about to rock his whole world on so many levels. His wife has no idea that he has two kids by me, and another on the way. It's all good because she's about to find out today. Rich is going to be pissed but why should I care, he been leaving for the longest and he still there. I'm just going to make it happen on my own." Keisha said.

"You sure that's what you want to do? Rich is going to be past pissed, and might not even speak to you after you tell his wife." *Chris knows me better than this.* If I say I'm going to do something, I'm going to do it. She should know that I already thought about that.

"Please, do you think he's worried about me? I only seen him twice this week and it was briefly. He came to drop off some *Pampers* for Lil Rich and left. Then he came over yesterday to drop off some milk and told me he would be right back. I'm still waiting on his right back! I'm tired of him and his little family over there when he's got one right here too. I'm sick of playing second when I belong in first place. I'm the one he runs to when shit gets tough over there. She's over there nagging him every five minutes about getting a job; I wouldn't do that to him. She knows damn well he's not working for nobody. She wants to change him, I accept him for who he is."

"Oh yeah, that's that bull right there! I thought he was leaving Dominique anyway? What happened to that?" *Now Chris was sounding like she was instigating. I'm already pissed; I don't need her adding to it.*

"He's been saying that since the day I met him. Talking about he wasn't happy and would be getting a divorce soon. Here we are, six years later, and you're still there? Oh trust me, he will choose today. I know how Dominique is; she's going to send him with his bags packing. He will have no other choice but to come here. I know damn well he won't be moving in with this new chick that he's out here prancing around." *Oh yeah Rich will be coming home to me even if it is forced. I want him here.*

"You do realize that if you tell Dominique all hell is going to break loose? How is that going to fly?" Chris questioned.

"Personally, I'm at the point where I just don't care how anything flies. They say that the truth will set you free. I warned him, I'm not living a lie for the rest of my life! I'm just going to tell her. I'm gonna be like, 'Look cuz, your marriage ain't what you think it is,' and just go from there." I walked out the bathroom and sat down on my crate that I use as a chair in the living room until I can get me some furniture.

"I'm sorry, Keisha, but I wouldn't do it. Some things need to stay in the dark." Chris said, sounding concerned about my situation. *I have already a made up mind. There is no talking me out of it.*

"Nah, I'm tired of not being able to bring my kids to the family gatherings because he's afraid of them calling him Daddy." I said shaking my head. "This is long overdue."

"Does your mother know about you and Rich?" Chris asked.

"Yeah she knows. I was staying with her when me and Rich hooked up. She caught me sneaking him in and out. That's why I went into the shelter for a little while when I was pregnant the first time, to hurry up and get my Section 8. I needed my own place so Rich and I could do what we wanted to do. My mother said if she caught us again she was putting me out. My mother went to my Aunts birthday party and saw Rich there with Dominique. That's when she put one and two together."

Chris is the first person that I actually told the story to. Everyone else I guess was too scared to ask me anything about my children's father. I am known for having a problem with my temper. Sometimes my hands just get to swinging.

"Wow, that's crazy! So that's how you found out? What did your mom say when she saw him?" *Now that I'm opening up, Chris isn't missing a beat.* She's my girl, I would have told her. All she had to do was ask me.

"Nothing, she was in shock. She told me to leave him alone, but I was already pregnant by then. It's just something that happened. If Rich had been honest from the beginning then we wouldn't be in this situation. I knew he had a girl and some kids, but I didn't know he was messing with my cousin. Then next thing you know, I find out that he married her." I walked back into the bathroom to mess with my hair some more. Carrying this baby was taking a toll on me; if I stand too long my legs swell up.

"I see this is messier than I thought. I still think that you should leave this alone. Just let it come out when the time is right. Dominique is going to be coming for your ass! You have to remember that you're still pregnant and in no condition to be out there fighting.*" I know Chris means well, and is only trying to look out for me. Pregnant or not, I'm no punk. I'm not saying that Dominique is either; I mean we do come from the same bloodline.*

"She better not. She knows better than to come over here. It is what it is. Her husband decided to cheat with her cousin because I make him happier than she does. She needs to just accept it and move on with her life." *I'm so serious, this has gone on long enough and if I wait for Rich to tell her, I'll be dead and gone. It's time for Dominique to wake up and recognize that her presence is no longer needed in my man's life.*

"I'm sitting here trying to figure out how she didn't know all of this was going on. I mean, both of y'all have sons named after him, only a month apart. If you were my cousin, I would have questioned you about your baby daddy. When he's not home where does she think he is? I mean New Haven ain't that big. Somebody had to see him creeping over at your house." Chris was sounding all puzzled. *Sometimes she can have an empty head.*

"He sneaks in and out. He parks her car around the corner and when she calls I let him answer the phone, because if I don't, then she will just keep calling. She a bug-a –boo. For real, I don't know how he puts up with her. They are always arguing because she thinks he's running the streets with his boys. She works third shift, so it's easy for him. Rich is a common name so she probably thinks that both our baby daddies share the same name." It ain't much to it. I made it easy for Rich, even if someone questioned our relationship I always covered for him. I would play the cousin's husband role quick.

"I'm not going to lie to you, but you are trifling as hell!" Chris started laughing at me. *I don't think it's funny. This situation is as real as it gets.*

"I know you ain't talking. How did you get with Poncho again? Please refresh my memory! Oh no, I remember…he was messing with Liz and then you came creeping in-between, knowing he had a girl. The pot is calling the kettle black!" Sometimes you have to bring a few things back to people's remembrance when they feel like they can throw stones.

"Oh no, we're in two different boats. Liz was not my family, and Poncho was not married to her. I didn't have any kids by him at that time." *Blah, blah, blah, this bitch is no better than me.*

"Rich wasn't married when I started messing with him either, and I already told you that I didn't know he was messing with my cousin. Stop trying to make it sound like your situation was better than mine. You got Poncho by default. If Liz didn't leave his ass, he wouldn't be over there with you!" Chris was plucking my nerves and they're already shot.

*****

I just keep looking at this picture of Rich and this new chick. *When I see her I'm going to whoop her ass, little does she know it. She looks like she's alright, but she has a fucked up shape; me and this chick don't even resemble. She's brown skinned, I'm dark skinned. She's flat chested and kind of skinny. I think she might be like an inch taller than me. I'm five-four, with a well-rounded body. What does Rich even see in her? Ugh, shit is pissing me off!*

*****

"If I found out that Poncho was messing with my cousin, please believe me when I tell you, the relationship would have been over. I might mess around with somebody's man, but it's never been a family member of mine." *Now Chris wants to throw shots. Truth be told, you can never be too sure of who the hell we sleep behind. People creep every day.*

"Yeah that's what you say now, but when your feelings get caught up, that's what it is! There is no on and off button. I was in love with the man by the time I found out, and I'm still in love. Plus, you're close to your family, I'm not!" *I can't seem to get this one piece of hair to lay down straight. I'm getting so aggravated. I also don't have the patience that I had with my other two pregnancies.*

"I hear you, but you still have another problem...this new chick." *Chris was rubbing this in. I want to say, 'The same way Poncho came to you is the same way Rich will come to me.'*

"I'm not worried about her, she don't hold no weight over here. Once he's here I plan on shutting all of that down. That mess that Dominique puts up with will not be me. He's not going to be able to get over on me when I know exactly how he operates." *Bitch, I'm not you! She still over there letting Poncho run all over her.*

"Yeah, I thought the same thing with Poncho, but he still finds a way to do his little bit of dirt. Well good luck, I have to get back in here to work. I'll call you when I get off...that's if you're still living by then." *Here she goes again laughing.* Chris thinks everything is funny.

"Oh, I'll be living. Bye. You just call me when you get off." *I'm not sure how Dominique is going to take this, but I want my man here with me. Let me dial these digits and let her know what's really up.*

*****

25

"Hello?" Dominique answered for me on the first ring like she was sitting by the phone just waiting on this call. She sounded like she was still sleeping. *Hmm she must have worked last night. That would explain why Rich was out hanging with that Ho!*

"Were you sleeping? I didn't mean to wake you." It just seemed like the right thing to say, but really I could care less.

"Who is this?" Dominique asked with straight up attitude.

"It's me, Keisha, your cousin." I replied sounding sweet as pie.

"I was, you don't call me. Is everything alright?" Dominique asked sounding worried.

"No, it's not. I have something that I need to tell you about your husband. Well, to make a long story short he's been cheating on us, he was out last night with some random chick that neither one of us knows anything about. We've been messing around for the last five years. Lil Rich and Richita belong to him. I'm also about to give birth to another baby. I know your mom told you that I was pregnant again."

CHAPTER 3

LIZ

"What's up Mika? You look a little worn out today." I said to my co-worker...well friend. Because even though we worked together, the two us developed a good friendship.

"Liz, I didn't get home until two-thirty this morning. I'm so tired; I don't know how I'm going to get through this day. Remember I was telling you about the new dude that I met? Well we went out last night. First, he took me out to eat at Captain Jacks in West Haven, then we took a stroll on the beach. It was so nice. From there he wanted to go have a drink, so we went to Ballards and danced the night away. He thought he was getting some; I had to put a stop to that. I was like, 'Slow down, I just met you!'" I just smiled because if a man does all of that for you, then yes, he's definitely expecting something in return.

"Well I'm glad you had a good time. You deserve it. You might be sleepy, but it's that good sleepy. When you get out of here take your butt home and get some rest. You have no kids, you can do that." *It feels good to see Mika happy for a change.*

"I wish, but I have class tonight so I can't go home and sleep. You must have forgotten." Mika reminded me. *I forgot her semester started up again.*

"Yes, I did. Oh well, after class go get you some rest." I said jokingly.

"I will. He wants to take me out again tonight, but I'm going to pass. He says he's going to give me back my money today though." *I'm almost afraid to ask, but I'll take my chances.*

"What money?" *I know Mika didn't give this man money already.*

"When he went to pay for the food his credit card got declined. Something about a hold on his account, so I just paid for everything. He said he was going to the bank today to get that straightened out." *Okay, so she paid for her own date...not cool at all.*

"Sweetie, when that card declined, that's when I would have jumped ship and let him sit right there and figure out how he was going to pay for that food. Then he had the nerve to want a drink when he knew he had no money. What kind of ghetto mess is this?" I can only shake my head at Mika. *I think she was born stupid for any man.*

"He said I'm getting it right back. I don't see the problem with it, so why should you?" I forgot how much Mika seems to jump on the defensive side instead of seeing things for what they really are. *Dumb move.* She won't see that money, and she still going to continue to date another bum. *Here I go again being the shoulder to cry on. I can already see it coming.*

"You're right; I was just trying to look out for a friend. It's not my money, so I'm staying out of it. I hope he gives you your money back." *I know when it's time to shut up, and that's exactly what I'm going to do.* I turned around and started doing my work.

*****

For the rest of the day I just stayed to myself typing away at my desk. Mika sits across from me, so it wasn't hard for me to see her texting back and forth with a case of the giggles.

She falls in love too quick. I've watched this girl get hurt over and over again because she will fall for any and everything these lame ass dudes tell her. *She's such an airhead.*

I'm older than her, so I try to tell her about these dudes but she doesn't listen to me. Poncho took me through the ringer until I finally got up enough nerve to leave him alone. In the ten years we were together there were countless women that he cheated with. Every time I turned around I was out in the streets fighting some chick over him. I thank God that I woke up, but that was after he made baby number seven on me. All seven kids have seven different baby mamas, and I fought each and every one of them. I'm the only one that has three by the dead beat; mine are all girls too.

I'm lucky that I made it out of that relationship without being HIV positive because he gave me everything else; herpes, warts, gonorrhea, chlamydia, trichomoniasis, crabs, and syphilis. I was always at the doctor.

Poncho never had a job in his life either. He didn't have to work; his women took care of him and me. I didn't realize it then, but he has nothing to offer anyone but a great lay in the bed. Silly me, I just knew I had something good in him, blinded by his dick and the long stroke.

I had to get myself together. He wasn't doing nothing but bringing me down. I was too busy chasing after him instead of taking care of myself.

Poncho wore me down to the point where I was sick. Ended up at Yale a few times from dehydration, not even realizing that I wasn't drinking fluids. I was the one running around here looking like a straight up crackhead. I was down to ninety-eight pounds, hair was falling out, face broke out, and I wasn't sleeping. I was just a train-wreck.

I got fired from good jobs because I couldn't even go to work. Half the time I was too tired from chasing him, the other half was because depression wouldn't let me get out of the bed. That's why I have a soft spot when it comes to females like Mika; don't be stupid like I was. It upsets me to see another female hurting behind a no good dude.

I became very distant from people throughout my relationship with Poncho. I stay to myself, go to work and come home. I don't fuck with nobody and I love it. I don't have to deal with fake and phony. So many people hurt me along the way. Smiling in my face, hanging with me, and they all knew what Poncho was doing.

Some were playing both sides of the fence, like that damn Dominique. We used to be real cool. I considered her my home-girl until I was riding down Dixwell Ave. one day, stopped at the light, pulled up beside her and she's chilling in the car with Michelle; one of the chicks that Poncho had a baby on me with. I honked my horn and gave her the head nod, letting her know I saw her. Her mouth dropped wide open. From that day forward I gave her my ass to kiss. You can't hang with me and her; my friendships don't go that way. Guess that's why I don't have any friends other than Mika.

*****

I've been working at this job, that God blessed me with, for the past two years and don't be bothered. I took to Mika when I caught her crying in the bathroom over Mr. No Good Number One. My heart wouldn't allow me to just leave her and her broken heart in there like that. I helped her get herself together that day and we've been cool ever since.

*****

Mika was in this 'so called' relationship, with Kyle for three years and had never been to his house. She never met any of his family, he never took her out, and she never even spent one holiday with the man...not even her birthday. He claimed he was so busy planning a future for them, but in all actuality he had a wife and kids at home. I think a ten-year-old could have figured that one out.

Any time a man can only see you at night, here and there, that's when you know he's hiding something. She got smart and started checking social media and that's how he got busted. She sent an inbox to his wife, sure enough the conversation started, and the truth came out. Mika was some kind of devastated.

I was surprised when she started messing with Mr. No Good Number Two; a jail-bird named Maurice, that one of her 'so called' friends, introduced her to. Mika was holding him down for a couple of months while he was promising her the world. Dude got released, and she hasn't seen him yet.

Then there was Mr. No Good Number Three. I call him 'The Charmer'. His name was Joe, some kind of entrepreneur on the come up. Had her thinking they were going to get rich and travel the world. He managed to drain her savings, and the whole time he was hitting the crack pipe. All she was doing was supporting a bad habit of his. Mika caught him in her apartment 'Beaming it up Scottie.' I kept trying to tell her, 'Don't give him any money.' She got mad at me and told me to mind my business, so that's what I did. Then one day a work she came crying to me telling me I was right once again.

Then there was Julian; the last one she was so head over heels for, and just knew he was the one. Well, come to find out, he was for everybody.

He had a chick on every side of New Haven. Driving by them telling them that it wasn't him, it was his twin brother that their eyes were seeing. I swear these dudes can come up with a lie quicker than you blink your eye. Guess who believed him? Mika did! Mika called herself throwing him a surprise birthday party at the Jump, which was his hang out spot, or so he said. That didn't go over too well. She ended up getting jumped by, I guess the main chick, his baby mama, and the rest of her crew. Mika had to take a week off from work. Her eyes were shut from two black eyes, a broken rib and sprained ankle. Now here she goes again getting herself into another mess. I can see a big, old sign saying 'Danger Zone, Do Not Enter.' But hey, who am I? I'm just a friend that cares, that's all.

I guess working and thinking paid off, because the day just flew by. *Time to go. I'm so ready to punch out, go home and clear my head.*

*****

"Hey, sorry if I was a little snappy at you earlier. I noticed you were really quiet today." *Here she goes; I'm not in the mood to talk right now. All I want to do is pick my kids up from the after school program and go home.*

"It was busy today; I had a lot of claims to catch up on. I don't want to see anyone take advantage of you. You already know my story; sometimes you can be very narrow-minded." Mika was walking with me to the time clock.

"I hear you, I really do. If he doesn't give me my money back it's going to be a problem, but I did have a really good time with him. He treated me like a real lady and it didn't seem like he had anything to hide. I just want to see where this can go." Mika said this about the last five bums that she dealt with. I saw where they took her...on my shoulder, in my arms, bursting into tears.

"Are you going to class tonight?" I asked Mika, because a lot of times she seems to get sidetracked when it comes down to a man. She's been doing well. After that last fiasco she had to drop her classes. Julian had her so traumatized that she was going to see a shrink.

"Yeah girl, tired and all, I'm going. I will see you in the morning, so we can do this all over again." Mika said sarcastically. She was getting tired of working here. She was starting to complain about this job daily, but for me it was a blessing. My bills were being paid, so that's all that mattered to me. Whenever they piss me off, I just think about my struggle and it straightens me right up.

"Yes, see you tomorrow. Have a good night." *I hope she gets some sleep tonight, but I'll find out in the morning. Oh Lord, Wanda is ringing my phone.* She's the gossip queen, so this means she has something to tell me.

*****

"Hello," I answered, trying to sound like I was in a rush. *I don't want to be on this phone with her too long.* Wanda can go on and on. Before you know it, it's been three hours.

"Girl, I was sitting here watching the clock, just waiting for five o'clock. Are you sitting down?" *She always asks me the same question.*

"I'm getting in the car now; I have to pick the kids up." I'm trying to give her a hint that requires her to hurry up with this gossip.

"Poncho is getting married on Saturday, girl...and it ain't to Chris." *I need for Wanda to repeat this.* "Are you there?"

"Yes, I'm here. The girls just spent the night over there with him and Chris last weekend. Are you sure that it's Poncho and not somebody else?" Wanda might be the gossip queen, but nine times out of ten, she knew what she was talking about.

"You remember Lisa McKnight, the chick we went to school with?" Wanda asked.

"Dark skin, kind of on the thick side?" I had to describe her to make sure she was talking about the same chick I thought she was.

"Yes girl! Well they been planning this wedding for a minute. It's going down on Saturday. A friend of mine has an invitation, and I'm going. I have to see this shenanigan of a wedding with love coming from one side, because we all know Poncho don't love nobody but himself. I can't figure out why these females even give him the time of day when they know he ain't shit." I guess Wanda called herself venting to me.

"Girl, you didn't know? These women don't have no respect for anybody's relationship. The women have turned into the new men. All they care about is getting what's in between their legs satisfied, attention seeking and hard up, that's what they are. The worse his reputation is, the more they get turned on. Now it becomes a competition because everybody thinks their pussy is better than the next chicks. Then once he dicks them down real good, now they got them lustful feelings that they have clearly mistaken for love. Next thing you know they want to be connected to the long stroke for life. The pills get missed, depo appointment is missed, and miraculously...the IUD comes flying out. Well now, nine months later here comes he or she because they think a baby will keep him. Ding Dong, the stupid bell rang. This is the oldest trick in the book. What worked in the fifties and sixties did not come into the twentieth century. Now they're caught up in the 'Baby Mama' club, getting the same thing we get; no man, a burning ass, no child support, few and far between visits, because he wants to play daddy when he feels like it. Then once they have completed the *Hooked on Phonics* course, all of a sudden the brain starts to work and here we go with the, 'He ain't shit syndrome.' Oh, and let me not forget the temporary case of amnesia where these chicks forgot all about how they ended up with him in the first place. You play dirty you get dealt with dirty. So when you go to this wedding on Saturday, give Lisa a big ole hug from me to her." *Yep I'm all in my feelings.* They thought they were taking something from me, when all they did was give me the best blessing ever...getting rid of him!

"Wow, you just said a lot. Round of applause is in order for you, my girly. Well you know I'm going to keep you posted with the details of this wedding, girl. I got my camera ready; I'm not trying to miss a beat. I told my girlfriend that I want to be the first one there to see who the hell is in this wedding. I can only imagine how Chris is going to feel about this." Wanda is dead serious. She will have that camera recording from beginning to end, and I will be the first person she shows it to.

"Well that one there, I damn sure don't care about! She knows that she shares him and she's okay with that; just like she told me, she's never going anywhere." *I remember it as if it was yesterday.*

"I don't know, Liz, this might be the deal breaker for her." *Wanda sounds so stupid, she's going to be hurt, but she will still be down for the cause when it comes to Poncho.*

"We will see, girl. Let me go pick up these kids. I will talk to you after this 'wedding of the year.'" I hung up the phone disgusted that these chicks haven't learned yet.

Any woman stupid enough to marry Poncho's dirty ass is a really special kind of idiot. How the hell do you marry a man that will never provide for you, and will always cheat on you, unless his dick happens to fall off? Marrying Poncho you might as well say you're paying to have a husband. *I hope this is not what the world is coming to. If that's the case, I'll forever be single with plenty of dildos to satisfy my needs. I'll be damned if I'm paying for a broke dick!*

CHAPTER 4

THE BUM SQUAD

PONCHO

I was posted up on Whalley Ave. waiting for the rest of my boys to arrive. I'm fresh out the barber shop with my clean cut standing up, hands in my *Tru Religion* jean pockets, one foot up against the brick wall to show off my fresh new pair of Nike's. I shined up my gold chain so that I would be beaming right along with the sun. A nigga was on it. As the ladies would say, I was feeling myself. Then Shawty walks by. She must have been impressed with what she saw. She walks straight up to me as I'm checking her out. She looks decent. Brown skinned, kind of thick, dressed pretty nice. I can tell from her t-shirt that she has a little belly, like most women have, but she ain't trying to hide it. No shame in her game. I saw her around a couple of times, but I never tried to holla.

"Hello," she says.

I nod my head still being the cool dude that I am. "What's up?"

"You look lonely, is everything alright?" She asked.

Now I'm standing here minding my business and this chick thinks I'm lonely. "I'm far from that. Just waiting on the rest of my crew to show up." *Don't she see what I look like and that I keep my body in tact?* My first stop in the morning is always the gym. I never have time to be lonely.

"No, I mean your eyes have a sense of loneliness in them." She said.

Okay, this chick is crazy as a bed bug. I don't really even know how to respond. I want to say, 'Bitch get the fuck out my face,' but I'm going to keep it cool and be the gentleman that I am. I let out a little chuckle. *She's funny to me.*

"Just what I thought. What's your name?" She asked.

"I'm Poncho, a well-known dude around these parts. What's your name stranger?" I asked, trying to be nice. She doesn't know we can cut all of this small talk and I'll give her what she really wants.

"Poncho, I've heard of you. My name is Honesty. I moved from Bridgeport not too long ago." *Damn, it's nice to know that she already heard of me.*

"I've seen you around, what's up with you?" I'm curious to know what this chick from the port wants with me.

"Nothing, I'm just trying to get to know New Haven. Are you attached, taken, or married?" Honesty asked.

I laughed. "According to me, or the streets, which answer do you want?" I asked.

"I want both answers, along with the truth. You laughed when I asked, what's so funny?" Honesty asked.

"You're so bold. Do all women from the Port act like you?" I asked. *This chick was live as hell. I'm kind of intrigued by her presence.*

"I'm not bold, just direct. I don't want to play in another woman's territory. If you have someone claiming stakes on you, then I will back up. Can you answer my question please?" Honesty asked in a demanding way.

I'm thinking she's very confident, because who told her that I even wanted her. "Well, according to the streets, I'm attached to a lot of women. According to me, I'm just a single man having fun. Did I answer your question?" I signaled to my boy Rich to hold up for a minute as he was walking up to me.

"Okay then, give me a call sometime because I'm a single woman doing me. I'm just trying to have a little fun and enjoy myself." Honesty opened up her pocketbook, grabbed a pen and wrote her number down on a piece of paper. She took it back to the old school and handed it to me.

I nodded my head as she walked away. Rich came walking up.

*****

"Yo, what the hell was that all about?" Rich asked giving me dap.

"It ain't nothing. It's just another one from the victims unit making a request." Rich and I both laughed. "What's up? Did you go rent that tux yet?"

"Nah, my bad. I was still waiting for you to call this off. You're really going to do this? Don't have me wasting my time and you choke up at the altar!" Rich asked sounding amused.

"Man, come on." I threw my hands up in the air. "You're my best man and you don't have your tux yet! I could understand if you had to pay for it, but man Lisa already paid for it! I need for you to take care of that! I'm dead ass serious; I'm doing it for real." *Rich should know me better than this.* I have never said anything about marrying a woman. I've been telling him about my wedding for a couple of months now.

"Why? What is the rush? I guess you moved out of Chris' place, right?" Rich asked, knowing damn well I didn't move anywhere.

"Nope, I'm waiting for the right time! We're not having any problems. Me and Chris are doing pretty good. She gives me my space. I want to stay cool with her. You know she has been holding me down." *Rich does this shit all the time. Always has to ask questions instead of just handling his business.*

"Stay cool? Man is you crazy? She's going to be hurt; you might be looking at a death sentence. You better get your shit out of her place and move while she's at work!" *I know Rich means well, but just shut the fuck up and let me do this.*

"To tell you the truth, I don't know how to tell Chris. I mean she's done nothing wrong at all to me. I can't even fake an argument right now. What you want me to do, just walk in there and say, 'Hey Baby; I'm getting married to another woman?' I can't do that!" The soft side of me was kicking in. I don't want to hurt Chris, but any way I do this, she will be hurt.

"Man, you better figure out something to tell her! I know you saying that y'all are on good terms and all but find something. All women can work a nerve. Strike up a conversation that turns into a big ass argument, and then get your stuff and bounce!" Rich suggested.

"What's the difference? She's still going to know that it was a set up when she finds out that I got married. Women are the best detectives ever made. They all belong on the police force. There wouldn't be any unsolved murders on the books! They can tell you where you were, the time, and the day!" *There's no way I can get out of this.*

"Yeah, you ain't never lying, but at least you wouldn't have to face her right away. You know how we do...run until you get caught!" Rich laughed. "Are you going on a honeymoon?"

"Yes, yes, yes! I'm going to be cruising for a whole week. I can't wait! At least I can cross this cruise off of my bucket list. I'll be doing two things that I've never did before. I think Chris will be alright after a little while. I mean she already knows that I'm not the faithful type. She might act like she doesn't know what's going on, but she knows. She's good to me, and a damn good mother to our son." I shook my head. "I think I'm just going to wait until I get back from the honeymoon. I figure the news will have broken by then."

"You straight tripping, Chris is going to cut your ass! You have to tell her; don't let her hear it from the streets! I bet she'll put you out then!" *I know this nigga ain't telling me about telling anybody anything when he needs to be a having a similar conversation with his wife.*

"Man Rich, on some real shit…you're the one with a whole family that your wife don't know nothing about! So before you come at me sideways, you need to handle your situation first, then let me know how that turns out!" I laughed at his ass, but of course he didn't find it funny. I know how to shut him up. *Yeah I got him thinking now.*

"Let me ask you this, why are you marrying Lisa? You've only been dealing with her for a few months and y'all already planned a wedding. What did you do, meet her and decide to go all in?" I like how Rich just went from one extreme to the other.

"Man, this is crazy how this happened. So this one Saturday I'm over there chilling on the boulevard, eating my breakfast sandwich, just scoping out all the women walking in and out of the flea market. Lisa comes up to me and hands me a flyer about her church revival and asks me to come out, hear a good word from the Lord and what not. I'm telling her that I will come, knowing damn well I'm not! Then she tells me she remembers me from high school; that she went to Cross too. I ended up standing out there talking to her for about an hour. Somewhere in the conversation I got lost and promised that I would show up. That Tuesday I held onto my promise for once and went. The whole time I'm in there, I'm just checking out the ladies. Man, I didn't even realize that it's a lot of fine women in the church. You have to check it out one day, I'm telling you, son. Anyway, long story short, after the service we talked some more, exchanged numbers, and we started hanging out. I'm feeling her, she's feeling me, and I can't get none. She tells me that unless I plan on marrying her, then I can forget it. I pay it no mind, 'Yeah, yeah, heard it all before,' type of shit. Two weeks later and I still haven't got close to them panties, a month later, same thing. So now I propose by mouth, a nigga ain't got no money for a ring. Nothing formal, just a, 'Let's get married then' because you ain't gonna keep getting my dick hard with no action. When I leave her I have to run home and bust off in Chris real quick. Well not quick, but you know what I mean. The next day she's planning a wedding! I'm still not thinking nothing of it until we start running around looking for flowers, picking out a cake, and rings. Then I say to myself, 'Oh this wedding thing is getting real serious.' Now I just know I'm going to get some. This chick thinks I'm really going to marry her! You know what I got, not a damn thing! There hasn't been a woman out here that I haven't been able to talk out of them panties. So yes, she's the one, and I'm getting married!" *Lisa was a challenge, and having me wait…that sweet spot better be all of that.*

"You know this has got to be the craziest shit that you have ever done. Where is the love at man? You're getting ready to take a lifetime plunge because you couldn't get the pussy! Do you know how many times I should be married then?" Rich was questioning my motive.

"Well I'm not you, and I haven't had that type of problem up until now. Women are thinking that they're not giving me none until I put that special touch on them, then it's all over. Plus it's my time to just pick one." *I have to get in Lisa's panties, and if marrying her is going to do it, then so be it.*

"Pick one? Nigga you ain't even dropped none, and from what I just saw, you are still picking! Don't do it man. I'm telling you!" Rich said.

*****

"Don't do what?" Quan asked as he walked up.

"I'm trying to tell Poncho not to get married. I'm married, living with skeletons that ain't dead! Shit tears me up on the inside every time I look at my wife. She doesn't even know who she's really married to. As much as I love her, I keep messing around. This head right here, over powers my brain." Rich grabbed his manhood. "Then I feel bad and go and do the same damn thing over again."

"Let this man do what he wants to do." Quan pointed at Poncho. "I'm looking at it like this, these chicks know how a nigga is already, so if they willing to accept it, then so be it! Your conscious is fucking with you because you're all up in the family! You're the one with kids by your wife's cousin! Poncho doesn't have that problem! Don't be putting off what's going on with you to the next man."

"I'm trying to save him from making the mistakes that I made. It's one thing to be messing around on your girl, but marriage is another world. Poncho isn't ready to be nobody's husband." Rich said.

"Yeah, whatever…marriage ain't nothing but a women's security blanket and a man's playground. These women are hard up and that's the only world we live in. Your dumb ass did that bid and came home with that jail talk, talking about getting married. You wasn't ready either, but couldn't none of us tell you anything. What did you say? 'I love Dominique. She held me down!' Remember all of that?" Me and Quan laughed. That's exactly what Rich said to us when we told him not to do it. "Anyway, I went and got fitted for my tux and so did Trey. We are ready for Saturday!" Quan assured Poncho, changing the subject, and getting back to the real reason they were hooking up in the first place.

"That's what's up! I'm glad somebody has my back. Where is Trey and Mickey anyway?" Poncho asked, staring at three random chicks that just walked by.

"Trey is tied up playing daddy daycare to some kids that don't belong to him, and Mickey said he was going to get fitted for his tux." Quan replied.

"Well I guess I'm the only one that needs to go then. I'm going to head out now fellas, and get this done and over with." Rich gave Poncho and Quan dap. "I guess we will hook up on Friday. We have to throw my homey a little something before he takes this plunge."

"Yeah Boy, that's what I'm talking about!" Poncho was all for that. "Oh Rich, before you leave I need for you to do me a favor. After the wedding I'm going to need you to bring my son back to Chris. You're going to have to change after the reception. Just tell her that I got tied up or something!"

"Alright man, I got you! I'll catch up with y'all later!" Rich said as he was walking off.

CHAPTER 5

KEISHA

"Girl what happened to your face?" Chris asked Keisha.

"It took you two days to get over here! I've been calling and texting you for two fucking days!" Keisha yelled.

"Uh excuse me, but my phone was off. It got turned off the same day that I talked to you. I've been helping Poncho pay off this bondsman so he don't get locked up. My money is really tight, so that's why I just decided to drop by." Chris said.

"Yeah, well the bitch came over here and caught me off guard! After I hung up the phone with you, I called Dominique to let her know the deal. I told her the whole nine yards and she was real calm about the whole situation. She told me how it was his fault and that she would deal with him. She kept saying 'My husband has two babies and one on the way by my cousin. Ha!' I kept the story moving because I wanted her to know the whole truth. When I hung up the phone with Dominique she was going to be putting him out her house! Girl, I haven't seen or heard from Rich!"

"Let me ask you again, what happened to your face? You look like you were in a fight with Laila Ali." Chris asked again.

"Oh yeah, she came over here! When I heard the knock on the door I just knew it was Rich coming to cuss me out, but it was Dominique coming to bum rush me! Girl, we were in the hallway rumbling like we were in a wrestling match. She picked me up twice and slammed my big ass on the floor! I didn't think she was capable of that! Everything just happened so fast. I think I must have blacked out at some point! My neighbor called the cops and her ass got locked up! Where do you think Rich is?"

"I'm not worried about Rich! You're pretty busted up, with a baby in your stomach! Did you go to the hospital once the cops came?" Chris asked.

"Yeah girl, I woke up at Yale New Haven Hospital! They wanted to keep me there for observation. I felt fine so I checked myself out. I wasn't sure if Rich would be knocking at my door or not! He has a key, but he never uses it…just in case somebody sees him. All I knew was that my man was finally coming home to me after all these years!" I couldn't help but to smile at the realization that we will finally be together. *I have been waiting on this day. Rich needs to hurry up and get here.*

"You checked yourself out? Are you crazy? We have no idea right now if this baby is okay or not!" Chris said concerned.

"This baby is kicking the shit out of me. Ain't nothing wrong! I do need your help though, I'm getting ready to take this corkscrew and bust open my membrane! I need to drop this load. This baby is taking too long!" The sooner this baby comes, the quicker I'll be able to handle all my unfinished business with these bitches. Dominique knows that if I wasn't pregnant she wouldn't have been able to knock me out. I plan on rearranging her face.

"Hell no, I don't want no part of that! You're talking reckless! I tried to tell you that this mess was going to backfire on you! You should have just let the truth come out however it was going to come out!" Chris said.

"It would have never come out as long as I kept my mouth shut! I had to throw the ball in my court! You of all people should understand!"

"Well I don't understand! Liz caught me and Poncho messing around! I never said anything until after she knew! She was the one that kept coming for me, calling my phone, coming up to my job, coming to my apartment, stalking me at my mother's house. She was a full time stalker. Every time I looked up she was staring me in my face. Now that's the shit I got tired of. Bitch wouldn't let me breathe! You took it upon yourself to call Dominique and tell her everything; that's a no, no! You're going to be lucky if Rich ever speaks to you!" Chris said with frustration.

"Oh, I have his kids. He has no other choice but to speak to me! Rich and I are tied for life!" *Who does Chris think she's yelling at. I haven't changed that much. She knows I can't control my fist when I'm pissed the hell off!*

"Keisha, you are not being real with yourself. Rich doesn't spend time with those kids or you! You really don't have a relationship with him outside of making babies. You're always calling him…it's one sided! The only time Rich even calls you is the first of the month, so he can borrow your food stamp card to feed his wife and kids over there!" Chris pointed her finger at me.

"See, because you think you got Poncho, you over there riding this white horse! You're trying to throw shit up in my face like you ain't been in my shoes! Bitch, we walking the same damn street! You got Poncho by default. Liz no longer wanted him. Rich may get some of my food stamps but that's about it! You're over there paying rent, lights, gas, cable, buying food, and giving him money! Your cell phone is off and his is on! Plus, you're taking care of a child that the two of y'all made together; but you want to come at me talking about a relationship being one-sided, like your shit is full-sided! You're paying for dick! Please, have several seats and find something else to come at me with!" Now I was letting Chris have it. *Always talking about somebody, like her shit don't stink.*

"Keisha, I didn't come over here to argue with you, but since you want to go there, we can! First off, yes, I pay all of my bills. I work and he doesn't! I was paying my bills before Poncho even got there. I've never been the type to sit around and depend on a man to take care of me! I'm going to always go get my own! You, on the other hand, have the community taking care of you! You're on

Section 8, getting a utility check and social services off of my tax dollars that I work for! Pushing out babies to try and keep a man that gave your cousin his last name! You and your kids are New Haven's best kept secret because very few even know that Rich even deals with you! You have nothing to even offer Rich; no job, no car, you don't even have furniture in here; there's an echo in here because it's empty, just like your brain! Rich would never leave his wife for a chick like you! Now you sit and marinade on that!" Chris said angrily. *I must have struck a nerve.*

"You can say what you want but I'm not taking care of Rich! When these kids need pampers or milk he goes and gets it! When I ask him for a couple of dollars to get some hair he gives it to me! What does Poncho give you? Nothing, that's what! All he does is take, take, take!" *I bet you the bitch don't have no come back.*

"Keisha, you have a nice life. I have a feeling that it's going to get a lot worse for you! The bottom line is that I'm in a relationship with Poncho and you're not in one with Rich! Whatever I choose to do for my man is my prerogative. That little twenty dollars that Rich gives you here and there to do your raggedy hair will never amount up to what you really want. You wish Rich would come live with you! Rich won't even take you out because he doesn't want to be seen with you. You can't say it's because he's married, when he was just out and about with the next chick! Now that says a lot to me! The fantasy that you're living in is never going to happen! You're never going to have the family that you want!" Chris said.

"So you say! And you're never going to have the family that you want either! If I were you, I wouldn't be over here talking shit to me! What you need to do is go and find your man that's about to be somebody's husband!" I was trying real hard to stay away from the rumor mill, but she pushed me.

"Girl, please!" Chris laughed. "Let me get away from your delusional miserable ass! Goodbye Keisha, you have a nice life!" Chris said as she walked out the door.

*****

She's laughing now, but she'll be crying in a minute. *Running around here thinking she's better than me. Oh no bitch, you're not!* Let's see what family she has after she finds out that Poncho is getting married. I always knew she was a little flaky; I should have never picked her back up! I'm just going to lay here and bust open this membrane so that I can deliver this baby and go find Rich myself.

*****

"Hey Baby," Rich said as he was walking through the door. "What's wrong with you?" I saw the look on Dominique's face, and if looks could kill, somebody would be dead on the spot.

"Do you know where I've been?" Dominique asked.

"I thought you were in this house sleeping. I had the car so why are you asking me a stupid question like that?" I was confused.

"Well, let me tell you. I've been on Union Ave., locked the fuck up!" Dominique yelled.

"What, for what? Why didn't you call me? I would have come home; I was only around the way with the fellas. What, you and the neighbor got into it again?" Dominique is always getting into with the neighbors over every little thing.

"No, this didn't have anything to do with the neighbor! I went around the corner and borrowed my mother's car because I had an emergency to take care of!" Dominique said, pissed the hell off!

"Tell me, what was the emergency that had my wife on Union Ave.? I told you before that your temper can be reckless! Now you have to go back and forth to court again! This time the judge probably won't throw it out! I hope Yale don't fire you because you done went out here and caught a charge!" *She knows damn well that I'm not working. If she loses her job behind some bullshit, then who in the hell is going to provide? I'm tired of checking her on her attitude.*

Dominique got up and walked straight up to me like I was the problem. *I didn't tell her to go and get locked up. I bet you been fighting somebody.* "When was my husband going to tell me that he fucked my cousin and fathered two bastards with one on the way? Ha, when were you going to tell me, and don't move bitch because I will cut the shit out of your neck! I was locked up behind your ass! I had to be bailed the fuck out. The whole time I was in there all I could see was your blood splattered all over this fucking house!" *Shit, who the fuck told her!*

"Who is telling you this information? They made a mistake; it's not me! I promise you, baby! They're just trying to break up what we have! When I find out who told you this shit, they will be dealt with!" I was shaking as I was looking at the sharp knife that was touching my throat. *Somehow I have to talk my way out of this or I'm going to be a dead man.*

"Keisha called me herself; this is not he said, she said! Are you trying to tell me that she's lying when she has an invisible baby daddy that nobody knows and a child named Lil Rich, just like our Lil Rich?" Dominique questioned me.

"Dominique please, just hear me out! It's not what you think. Whatever she told you is a bunch of lies! Keisha always had a thing for me! I don't want Keisha, baby. I love you!" I said, stuttering and trying to think quickly.

"Now you're trying to make me cut you! You love me so much that you would lay down with my own flesh and blood. Not only did you lay down with her, but you made not one, not two, but three babies! She's not even some random chick, Rich! How could you do this to me? I'm your wife!" I never saw Dominique like this, and now the tears were rolling. *I just might have to kill Keisha for this shit right here.* I might be a fuck up, but I love my wife and I can't stand to see her cry. *I wish she would have called or texted me, then I wouldn't have come home at all. Now I know why Keisha was blowing me up.*

"Please put down that knife! I'm so sorry, but we can get through this. I made a mistake!" I had to come somewhat clean. *I'm just watching this knife, one wrong move and that's my throat.*

"A mistake? Really? So you're trying to tell me that you mistakenly stuck your dick up in a dirty ass pussy...raw!" Dominique yelled. *I feel like I'm about to piss on myself.*

"Dominique, please put the knife down! I'll tell you everything you want to know!" *Think quick, Rich! This is one time things will not go in my favor.*

"Oh, I know enough! Keisha barely washes her ass, the bottom of her feet are black because she walks around the neighborhood with no damn shoes on, with a comb stuck in her head! She's known as 'Dirty Keisha,' and you fucked that! That's what you wanted, huh Rich? Answer the fucking question!" *How the hell am I supposed to talk with a knife at my throat?*

"No, that's not how it happened! I got drunk and fell asleep. She raped me!" *I think this is the quickest lie I ever told, but Keisha did take advantage of me that first night. It's kind of the truth.*

"She raped you?" Dominique laughed as she put the knife down. *Thank God, I just might make it out of here alive.* "I guess she raped you three times, that we know of! You must think I'm some kind of fool! You get drunk, get raped, and go back over there to get raped again! I don't know anybody that likes getting raped! Where is the police report? How come she's not locked up? Why wouldn't a husband come home and tell his wife? This has got to be one of the worst lies you've ever told! What made your stupid ass think that I would never find out?"

"I wasn't thinking; she's just trying to mess up our family. Keisha really did take advantage of me! You know how trifling your cousin is! First, I have to get a DNA test done to see if those kids are actually mine." *I had to pull out the 'I am not the father' card. I'm just hoping that it helps me, even if it's just a little bit. All I see right now is Keisha, six feet under.*

"Oh, they're your kids. You don't need a DNA test because you're the only the nigga in New Haven that would be stupid enough to run up in that! You know what I didn't realize Rich? I didn't realize just how trifling my husband is! Stupid me, Stupid me!" Now Dominique was walking around circling me.

"Not true, I swear she wasn't a virgin. She probably has quite a few dudes. I'm sure I wasn't the only one! I promise you, I will never be bothered with Keisha again. Whatever she was thinking was going on between me and her will not be going on anymore, I promise you that! That bitch can't even look my way and fuck those kids too!"

"Just shut the fuck up, Rich! I already knocked that bitch out, so now I'm trying to figure out exactly what I'm going to do to your bitch ass! I can't kill you; then the kids are left with a mother in jail and a father in the dirt! You're really not worth me catching another charge! I already have to go to court for assaulting a pregnant woman, trespassing, and some more shit! I'm going against everything that I'm feeling right now, but my two reasons for living are more important and they are the only reason why I'm not going back to Union Ave.!" Dominique was reasoning with herself. *I want to let out a sigh of relief, but that will definitely get me cut.*

"Dominique, baby, we can get through this! Love conquers all. I don't want to lose you; you are my everything! We've been through too much to throw it all away now!" I'm trying to plead my case.

"You have fucked up to the tenth power. There is no way in hell that I will ever stay with you! You just threw everything away for a broken-down bitch with no job, no car, and no nothing! I'm out here busting my ass to take care of this family and you out here running around, creeping while I'm at work! Well you two nothing having asses can have each other. I'm so done! Get all of your stuff and get it the hell out of my house!"

"I don't want her; I want you and you only. Keisha was just a very bad dream that I was in. If you need some time away from me then I'll give it to you, but what about us being that ride or die couple? Remember we used to always say that? I know we can get through this storm together." *If I have to beg for my marriage, then it is what it is.*

"You better get your ass out of here, or you can take a chance of not waking up in the morning, because I will kill you in this bitch tonight! Take your ass across town with your girl and her kids! I'm sure she's waiting on you!" I just want to hug Dominique and cry in her arms, but I know she won't let me touch her right now.

"I'm not trying to lose my wife and kids! Dominique, let's just go for counseling. You're giving Keisha what she wants! I know for a fact that the only reason she told you was so you would put me out!" *Keisha has another thing coming if she thinks I'm coming to her. It's over for real now; I'll never touch the bitch.*

"Counseling, Nigga are you serious? There isn't a counselor on this earth that can convince me to stay with a low-down, dirty dog like you! You did exactly what you wanted to do…lose me forever. Had it been any other bitch I might consider counseling, but you dug down real deep when you cheated with my family. The only reason why she told me was because she heard you were cheating on her with some other chick. Not only is there dirty Keisha, there's someone else too. Aww hell naw, you got me all the way fucked up! Take your ass right over there with Keisha's nasty ass and her nasty ass house to match!"

"Dominique, our kids deserve to see their dad every day. They're used to it! You're going to hurt them by putting me out! Please, just think about them! If you want me to sleep in the guest room then I will do that! Just tell me what I can do to fix this! Please don't give up on us!" Now I'm really begging.

"There is no fixing this; you can't fix things that are broken! I'm beyond repair, Rich! What were you thinking? You should have thought about all of this before you stepped out on me and made babies! We live in a world where condoms do exist! No wife should ever have to deal with a baby because her husband should have so much respect for his wife that this doesn't happen! I really thought that we were past the cheating stage. I thought you changed and that I could trust you again!" *Dominique was really making me feel like shit.*

"I'm going to get myself together and give you everything that you've ever wanted. You just watch me! I'm not going to lose you Dominique; you say this now, but I can get you to change your mind! You nor these kids will never want for anything!" *I mean every word that I'm saying. I can't talk about it; I have to be about it.*

"First thing in the morning, Rich, I'm going to be at legal aid and the courthouse. I want a divorce with quickness, and then I'm going to my GYN Doctor and getting checked out. I just feel so dirty."

I could tell from the look on Dominique's face that I better get out of here. I went and packed my clothes. I was sure to leave some behind just to have an excuse to come back. Dominique handed me a black trash bag, she wasn't letting me use luggage bags. I called my brother Rob to come and pick me up. *This heartbreak right here is worse than death itself, I'd rather be dead than to be forced to live without my wife and kids. I did this to myself, and my family.* I guess I just took Dominique for granted by thinking that she was always going to be there for me. I think this time I broke her, but rest assured, I'm going to do everything possible to win her back.

"I'm leaving, Rob is here. Are you sure that this is what you want to do?" I had to ask one more time. Dominique was sitting on the couch crying. *I'm hoping that she don't want me to go.*

"Did you give me a choice? You took all my choices away from me! Do you think I'm going to walk around here married to a man that has made a fool out of me? How do you think I'm going to feel after I tell my kids that their cousins are also their brother and sister? Do you think I'm going to run around small ass New Haven being laughed at and talked about?"

"Please don't tell the kids that! I'm not sure if those kids are mine or not! For all I know they could be somebody else's. I wasn't there like that! We can move out of the state if you're worried about people finding out." *I'm getting a blood test done on all three of them babies. I hope they all come back not belonging to me, but the way my luck is, I am the father.*

"I'm not running because I married the scum of the earth. You know damn well those kids are yours! Have a nice life, Rich, and I'll see you in divorce court!"

CHAPTER 6

LIZ

$\mathcal{I}$ was sitting at my desk when Mika rolled up on me like the police. "Girl, I have to talk to you now!" *She comes in late and has the nerve to want to talk.*

"Okay." I got up from my desk and walked into our sometimes hiding space, the storage closet, where we could get some privacy. "What's up?"

"Liz, you are not going to believe this! So this new dude, Rich, that I met gets into it with his sister. She throws him out because she was stealing his money and he called her on her bullshit. Now he's at my place with all his stuff! Girl, you know that I never lived with a man before. What am I supposed to do?" *Oh no, I can't believe Mika let this man, that she barely even knows, move in with her.*

"Rich? What is his last name?" I asked because all the one's I know ain't about shit!

"Girl. I don't know. I'll have to find that out later when he picks me up!"

"Wait a minute, let me just make sure that I'm hearing you correctly. You have a man in your house that you don't even know his last name; to top it off he has your car! Mika, are you crazy? You don't even know him. Oh my God!" *I just can't with her. Why does she always set herself up for disaster?*

"What was I supposed to do, leave him sitting on Whalley Ave., homeless?"

"Uhh, yes. I'm sure he has family or a homeboy he could have stayed with! That man could be robbing you blind, and you don't even know if he's going to pick your ass up! He might just steal your damn car!" *Let me calm myself down. This is just another hard lesson she's going to learn.*

"Girl, I know, but he's there now and I'm kind of excited to have someone to come home to. It's lonely living by myself. See, at least you have your kids to keep you occupied!" Mika said, sounding like a pathetic fool.

"Let me tell you something Mika, I get lonely just like you. My kids can never fulfill the role of a man, but I'm not settling because I've already done that, and that man could have cost me my life! You don't meet somebody and in the same week move him in. When or if he picks you up, tell him he has to go! Does he even have a job?" *I'm afraid of this answer.*

"He's in between jobs right now. He was living off of his savings, but his sister took that. That's why he dropped me off; so he could go look for a job." *Another one that can't even pay his way. Dude will be living off of her for a good while. I can see it coming.*

"Well what happened to his car? I thought he drove the other day!" *Let's see what lie he told her.*

"It was in his sister's name so she kept it. His sister is a wicked witch! How could she do that to her own brother? I felt so bad for him." *I smell straight up bullshit.*

"Mika, listen to me, you are moving way too fast, sweetie. This sister could be an ex-girlfriend. This story doesn't sound right! Is his sister on drugs or something?" I'm trying to reason with her. If you know you have a track record of playing the fool, you would think that this time around she would be a lot more cautious.

"Good question, I never asked him, but you can meet him when he comes to pick me up. I want to know what your first impression is." Mika said, as if I don't already have my opinion. *I don't like dude already, meeting him will not change a thing.*

"It will have to be another time; I'm leaving early today to take the kids to the doctor. I have something to tell you real quick. The other day Wanda called me with some scoop and told me that my ex was getting married. The joke is that it's not to Chris. It's to this other girl that we went to school with."

"What? Oh my God! Girl, why didn't you call me as soon as you found out? Wait, let me skip over the gossip part, how do you feel about him getting married?" Mika asked; concerned about my feelings, in which I really don't have any. *I pity Lisa for marrying him.*

"Mika, I felt nothing pertaining to me. He got married on Saturday. You know Wanda couldn't wait to send me the pictures and she posted the video on the book. However, I feel bad for Chris, and I know that I shouldn't, but I do! Regardless of what she did to me when I was with Poncho, I know that she loves him and she treats my kids well! I also feel bad for his wife. I don't know her personally, but we went to school together and she was always on the quiet side. This is going to be interesting as to how this turns out."

"I'm so glad that I don't know your baby father! He's an accident waiting to happen for any female. Does this Chris chick know yet?" Mika asked.

"Oh I'm quite sure she does by now. I started to reach out to her, but decided to just leave it alone." *I'm minding my business like I always do, ain't nothing changed.*

"Well anyway, enough of that, do you want to hang out this weekend? Newt's is going to be popping. They're having a party for all the bikers. I figured we could make it a girl's night out; all you do is go to work and go home. You need to get your life girl!" *I guess this was Mika's way of telling me that I'm an old dud. She knows I don't go out.*

"I don't know…I'm just not into the party scene. Why can't we go out to eat or something?" *The last place I want to be is in somebody's club with a bunch of drunken ass people making fools of themselves.*

"No, we are not going out to eat. I want to see some men, get my dance on, and have a few drinks. You need some fun and action in your life. You can't live your life through your girls forever. Every time I ask you to go out, the answer is always no. You always have excuses. Are you ever going to date again? I think it's time, now that you have turned into a virgin all over again!"

They both laughed.

"You know what's crazy? It's been two years and I'm still not ready. I didn't even realize it, until you just asked me. In order for me to be ready, I would have to be open to being hurt again and I'm not." I cringed at the thought.

"Who says that you're going to get hurt? This next man could be your everything! You see me, I'm never giving up on love. I know that my special someone is out there. That's why I keep trying, no matter how much these men have hurt me. I've ran into every asshole that you can think of. I use your shoulder to cry on and ear to vent to, get over it and move on to the next. You can't win if you don't try. It's time for you to be happy, Liz. Get out of the house, come have a drink, and get your dance on." Mika was being very pushy, a little out of her character, especially when it comes down to me. Usually it's me getting on her.

"Girl, I don't want to be like you; getting hurt every five minutes...my heart can't take that! I don't know how you do it. I don't believe anything a man says. When they try to holla, I just keep on moving! All men are full of shit! I'm going to go out with you, but I'm not looking for any man, just going to have some much needed fun." *I can't believe I agreed to do this.*

"Alright girl, I'm holding you to it!" Mika said with excitement grinning from ear to ear. *I guess I made her day. Maybe she will cancel since she now has a live in.* That's how chicks get when they have a man living with them; everything comes to a stop! *I'm just wishful thinking. Knowing Mika, we are going out.*

"We have to get out of this closet. I have to clean off my desk and pick my babies up to take them to their appointment. I guess I will see you tomorrow night!" I said, trying to hurry up before I don't make it out of here in time.

"There is no guessing, tomorrow night, it is! Tell the girls mommy's going to be a grown up this weekend!" Mika was laughing.

CHAPTER 7

THE AFTERMATH

PONCHO

"You think that you can walk in here, nigga, like you ain't get married? Like I'm supposed to be cool with it." Chris was irate. If I didn't know any better, I would think that she could kill me. She ran up to me punching, screaming, and kicking me. I had to pin her down so she could gain some control over herself.

"Listen, get yourself together. I am not your punching bag." *I don't like having to man handle a woman. This is not my style at all. She's not even trying to be reasonable. What the hell she hitting me for?*

"Get the fuck off me!" Chris yelled.

"I can't let you up until you get that fire out of your eyes. I understand that you're hurt and I'm sorry." *Chris is out of control.*

If I would have known it was going to be like this, then I would have done what Rich told me to do; just pack up, leave, and hide out until I was found.

"You're right; you are a sorry ass motherfucker!" Chris was breathing really hard; she was out of breath from trying to get me off of her.

"Calm down baby girl, it ain't that bad. I'm here right now." *If I can get Chris to calm down a little bit, maybe she would understand that I didn't get married to leave her. We can still be together; I just have to go home at night.*

"Nigga, it's over! Do you understand me? Over, Over, Over!" Chris was crying uncontrollably.

"I know what you need, you need daddy to give you a little bit and kiss that sweet spot!" *Maybe if I give her some. It has been a week. I did hit her off the night before the wedding.*

"You sick ass bastard. I'll let a bitch fuck me before you ever touch me again!" Chris screamed.

"I like when you're mad at me, it just does something to me. I think it's sexy as hell!" *Make up sex with Chris was always the best.*

"Poncho, I'm going to give you three seconds to get your cruddy ass off of me!" *I'm going to get up off of her even though I know she really don't want me to.* As soon as I got up Chris went to swinging again.

"Look now, cut it out!" Now she was starting to piss me off. *I can't go home to my wife with a bunch of scratches and bruises; how am I supposed to explain that?*

"You went and had a whole wedding and put my damn son in it! Then you have the nerve to walk your ass in here like it is nothing!" Chris was still yelling at the top of her lungs.

"It's our son; yes he was the ring bearer. If I would have told you, then you wouldn't have let him be in the wedding! It's no big deal. Me being married don't change nothing. I'm still going to be over here! You're mad over a piece of paper, come on now, Chris!" I was trying to assure her, but the more I talked, seems like the madder she got.

"Somewhere in your sick, twisted mind you really believe what the fuck you are saying! Another bitch gets to walk around here with your last name! Motherfucker, I thought I was helping you pay off a bail bondsman. I went without, and the whole time I was really helping pay for a fucking wedding that I wasn't the bride of! You lying bastard! I knew you could be low, but even I didn't have you digging down this fucking low! I underestimated you!" Chris said angrily.

"I can't say nothing on that, but this is why I didn't tell you. I guess I underestimated you too. I didn't think this would be your reaction. I knew you would be mad, but not this mad! I need for you to be okay with a decision that I made." *I thought Chris would be more understanding. Now I have to hear, 'I told you so' from Rich!*

"I haven't been to work all week long because I'm sick to my stomach! Nigga, you could eat my shit and it still wouldn't be good enough for me! Do me and you a favor; get the fuck up out of here! If we ever cross paths again you better walk on by like you don't even know me, because if you even utter one word to me, nigga, it will be your last! As far as our son, nigga, you just minus one! You don't do shit for him anyway! You and your dusty ass wife go have a nice, miserable fucking life! Leave my damn key!" Chris threw the picture of us together that was hanging on the wall.

"Oh, I'm going to see my son. You making a big deal out of nothing! What you need, a couple of weeks to calm down?" I asked.

"Poncho, get out and go home to your wife! I'm moving and changing my number. You won't know where I live at; I'm cutting off all ties with you! When my son asks about you, I'm going to tell him, 'Daddy is dead and gone!' I'll find him a father, but it damn sure won't be you!"

"Chris, don't get stupid. You knew you weren't the only woman that I was dealing with. You came to grips with it a long time ago!" *I'm trying to figure out what this behavior is all about! I don't like setting a woman straight, but I will if I have to. She knew damn well it wasn't just about her. I'm not even going to try and sugar coat it.*

"Cheating on me and getting married on me are two different things! It wasn't even like we broke up, nigga. We were still together when you went and said, 'I do,' to the next bitch!" Chris started throwing shit everywhere.

"Chris, you're blowing this out of proportion!" I went in the room to pack my things and to my surprise all my stuff is gone. "Chris, where's my clothes?" I walked back into the living room where Chris is balled over on the couch crying like somebody died. "What did you do with my clothes?"

"What clothes? You mean the clothes that my money paid for, the shoes and sneakers that my money paid for? You don't get to take shit out of here! I held everything down in here; you didn't contribute shit!"

"Thank you for everything that you've done. Do you want a medal for it? Where did you put my stuff?" I asked. Now I have an attitude, and I don't even care about her tears or the shit that she broke up in this apartment.

Chris laughed. "Well the trash man came this morning, so all your stuff is at the motherfucking dump!"

"You know how I feel about my clothes; I can't believe you threw my shit out!" I began to pace back and forth, trying to keep my hands up off of her.

"I see why Liz didn't want you anymore. I just had to be the stupid one to take your bum ass in! When Keisha mentioned something to me about a wedding, I laughed in her face! I thought she was being delusional. In my mind, I just knew that you would never get married to anybody other than yourself!" Chris said, looking at me in disgust.

"Oh, I go with the best offer. Juggling women is like a job to me. Anybody with common sense is going to take the job that pays the best and has the most benefits. That's what I did, and you're mad at me?" All I want Chris to do is go along with the program. There's something in this for her too, if she acts right.

"This just gets better and better! She must be paying you very well. Wait until she finds out the truth. Let's see what happens then! The highest bidder wins with you; love doesn't have anything to do with it!" Chris screamed.

"Nothing is going to happen. She's going to think that you're bitter, and she'll take her husband's side. Love crossed my mind, but I had to do what was best for me. When the opportunity knocks, you have to grab it while it's there! Now I need a whole new wardrobe. The only clothes I have are the ones that I took on the honeymoon." *She really got rid of my stuff. I was still looking around thinking that maybe she was bluffing; guess not!*

"Well, let her buy you some, I'm sure she can afford it. She might not believe me at first, but as time goes on, she'll know that I was telling her the truth. I took on Liz's problems and now she's taken on mine. Poncho, you are nothing but a big ass problem that can't be solved!" Chris said shaking her head.

"You're acting like this is the end of the world. How many times do I have to tell you that I'm not leaving you! You held me down and I could never forget it! I'm still going to be around!" *It's just going to be a little change, but Chris is acting like she don't understand English.*

"Let me tell you something Poncho, you married that chick as a business investment, but I'm here to tell you that you got some hell to pay for, that no bitch can dig you out of! You can dig in all the pussies in the world, and not one of them pussies will help you from feeling the wrath! Now karma just caught up with my ass and I will endure this pain, because I deserve it from the dirt that I've done! This ride right here has been a learning experience for me, and you were a mistake that I promise will never happen again!" Chris was pissed.

"Chris, you ain't preaching a sermon that I haven't heard before. After all these years I feel like I'm still living in heaven. So what, I lose you then I just go out here and find a replacement! It's different for us men when we are not emotionally tied to a female. It's just like the boxers that I change every day! I don't sit around and cry over spilled milk, I just go buy another carton! I'm always amazed at females that think, like you, when you cheated with me! I didn't deliberately go out here and hurt you; you hurt yourself by thinking that you had me!" See, now I had to say what I was thinking but I didn't really want them words to come out my mouth, but she came at me in the wrong way.

"Do us all a favor and drop dead somewhere! GET THE FUCK OUT AND NOW!"

"Okay, I'm going. No hug, no kiss, no nothing! I'll hit you up in a couple of weeks to see how you're feeling!" I walked out the door in disbelief. *Chris is tripping. She needs to get her mind right.*

CHAPTER 8

THE BUM SQUAD

RICH & QUAN

"Yo Rich, have you seen Poncho since he been back?" Quan asked.

"No, we're supposed to hook up today. He said he had a nice time on the honeymoon though!" I replied.

"Yeah, I'm trying to hear all about it. She took my man on a cruise, I hear that shit! That's what's up!" Quan said boasting.

"I want to take Dominique on a cruise as soon as I get back in. I can't wait to give her the world! She deserves it, after all the shit I put her through! Man I'm so hurt right now, I just want my wife back! If she asked me to kiss this ground that we're standing on, I'll do it!" Mika is helping me get through this dark time. She's not Dominique, and all I want is her and my kids.

"I been meaning to ask you, what the fuck were you doing messing with black ass feet Keisha in the first place? Please tell me how the hell that happened? Don't get me wrong, her body is sick and her face is alright, but she dirty as fuck!" Quan was laughing his ass off.

"Don't get me started on that bitch. The less I hear her name the better! It's just something that happened, that's all!" *Quan sure knows how to mess up the mood. Keisha is the last person that I want to talk about.*

"Well you know she dropped that other load! She has been riding the bus all around New Haven looking for you, with a newborn baby! All them germs and stuff, you better go over there and holla at her! A bus ain't no place for a newborn! She should be in the house healing for real!" Quan said with concern.

"Fuck her and her kids! She knew the deal, and she got exactly what she wanted, which was for Dominique to put me out! The joke is on her. She wrapped that whole situation up for me. I was already stepping back once I saw that new baby bump! She didn't even tell me she was pregnant again. I had to find out on my own! Man was I pissed; I haven't touched her in months because of it. She made it seem like we were in some kind of relationship. I'm gone man, I'm gone!" *Keisha don't have nothing coming. Looking for me is her worst mistake.* I've never put my hands on a female before, but if I was to see her right now, I would knock the bitch out!

"Aww hell naw. That's what you should have done before you went and tapped that ass!" Quan laughed. "Now you want to run...three babies later?"

"I don't have any words for her. I can't even get Dominique to answer the phone for me. She changed the locks to the house and everything." I got some money from Mika the other day, so I brought Dominique a dozen red roses, tried to leave them in the house, but when I tried my key, it wouldn't open the lock. I went around to the back door and the same thing happened. I just waited until later on when I knew she would be at work and left them on her car in the garage. Sometimes she goes out to her car on her break. *I hope she got them.* When I call her all I get is the damn voicemail.

"From what I see, you okay. You are riding around in Shawty's car." Quan pointed at Mika's car. "She gave you a place to stay, so you're not homeless. You're not getting Dominique back. You can just get that out of your head."

"I'm getting my wife back! Nigga, I ain't you!" *Quan don't want me to get started.* He's the one that can't get, not one chick back. All the years I've known him he's never been able to.

"Well I'm not married, so I don't know what you mean by that! Listen here man, you stepped in some shit that you can't get out of for the rest of your life. You think that your wife can just overlook a triple threat. Those babies are constant reminders that her husband had another life going on outside of her. Now you know Dominique on an intimate level, and I know her as being my cousin! Keisha is a cousin that nobody claims. This is probably going to be the last time you hear me say that! Don't get me wrong now; she's cool as shit, but she's just entertainment. We don't invite her to family affairs because we never know how she's going to show up! When she shows up it's because she found out by accident. She will embarrass you real quick. Her clothes are dirty, she got that five-dollar weave in her head, and she doesn't believe in shoes. The only time them feet be clean is when she's walking in the snow. Why do you think that you didn't know that we were all related? All the years we've been hanging together, you ain't never heard me talk about my cousin named Keisha!" Quan said.

"I know I fucked up! Why you think I didn't tell you I was creeping over there? The only person that knew was Poncho, and that's because he caught me creeping out of her house. He just happened to be next door handling his business with her neighbor. It's not something that I'm proud of! If there were one thing that I could take back, it would be her. I was drunk as fuck!" *I really want to knock myself upside the head. I'm getting tired of my boys throwing it up in my face.*

"Drunk ain't even an excuse for her. It must have gotten real good to you for you to keep going back. It wasn't like it was a one-time deal!" Quan threw his hands up in the air.

"Look man, she washed her ass when she knew I was coming through! I didn't have those kinds of problems! Keisha is a freak. She'll do anything you want her to in the bedroom. If y'all wasn't related and you went over there, your ass would go back too!" *I do miss some of them tricks that Keisha pulled, but every time I looked at her stomach my dick wouldn't even get hard.*

"Nah, you wouldn't catch me over there messing up my rep. I got standards to live up to!" Quan was nodding his head, no.

"What standards? Nigga please! When Tisha's lights got cut off, you hauled ass until she got them shits turned back on! She's stupid for letting you back in. You was supposed to ride that out right with her." *Now I'm throwing shots back.*

"Sure did, a nigga needs to be able to see. We are talking two different standards here. Yes, I have standards for that kind of stuff too. She must have her own place, with all the utilities on; I need my cable. She must have food; a nigga needs to eat! She can't be skinny or thick; I like my women big! She has to have a clean house and wash her ass on a daily! Hygiene is an absolute must! She can't just jump in the shower because she knows I'm showing up! I'm not hitting no stinky pussy, not me bro! Soap, water, and deodorant, go a long way!" Quan said adamantly.

"You stupid," I laughed. "You need to find you a woman with a job that can help your crazy ass."

"Aww hell nah, let the government take care of us! Then I would have to hear her mouth about me not working, this way we equal. I just give up my food stamps every month and Tisha is happy with that! These other women want me to take them out and they try and dig in these empty pockets of mine." Quan said taking out his pants pocket.

"You talking about me; you are trifling as hell!" I had to laugh, Quan is a real funny dude and he's serious as hell.

"I'll take that charge; I'm not in denial. I'm well aware of me! I wish I could say the same thing for some of my crew." Quan looked over at me. "When's the last time you had a job? More like never."

"I'm looking for a gig; I put in a few apps this week. I'm trying to go home, but I know I have to come correct!" *I can't wait to go to work and let Dominique know that I have a job. A steady paycheck coming in will show her that I'm not just talking, I'm doing.*

"Rich, if you were trying to come correct you wouldn't be driving around in another woman's car and living with her! You are not a man acting like he wants his wife back." Quan pointed at Rich's chest. "What are you going to do when Dominique finds this out? You're adding more fuel to the fire!"

"Dominique knows about Shawty because Keisha let that out the bag too, with her big ass mouth, but I'm hoping she don't find out that I'm staying there. My plan is to get on my feet, then bounce from Shawty's place. She's just my in-between stage. I like her; she's good people, and a nice young lady, but she's not my wife."

"You need to go stay with Rob, at least make it look good, like you're free and clear. I keep trying to tell y'all playas that New Haven ain't that damn big. She's bound to find out! Nobody listens to me!" Quan pointed his fingers at himself.

"Rob got my back. If Dominique asks, then he knows to say that I'm staying over there. See, I'm ahead of you. Already got that situation taken care of. I have to go and pick Shawty up from work. I'll holla later!" Rich gave Quan dap goodbye.

CHAPTER 9

LIZ

I had a ball hanging out with Mika the other night. It gave me life; I haven't been out in soooo long. I actually forgot how much fun it could be.

My mom kept the kids, which is something that she rarely does, but I guess even she was happy to know that I was doing something for me. I was never the type to really hang out in bars or clubs, so when people saw me, they were in shock.

The music was right and the attention that I was receiving was very pleasing to me. Every time I would walk up to the bar to buy myself a drink, some dude would pay for it. Me not having to spend any money was an added bonus. I had plenty of conversations, exchanged numbers with quite a few dudes. A couple of them I knew; old bug-a-boos from back in the day that were still willing to try.

My little black dress complimented my petite figure just right, because they were on it. Plus the fact that I was considered a 'new face' from the regulars, paid off. Even after the bar, Whalley Ave. was lit, so the party continued in the parking lot. Dudes were out there flexing; everyone was standing by their cars with the music blasted, and every bike club in New Haven must have been out there showing off in packs, riding up and down the street.

I was standing in the parking lot just scoping out all the scenery when one of the dudes from the bar rolled up on me with his bike, looking sexy as hell. My body could have melted just from looking into his pretty brown eyes. I gave him a cute little smile, trying to hide what was really going on inside of me. I hadn't been with a man since Poncho, and thought I lost my desire, until I felt the wetness that was going on in between my legs. A bitch was horny and could very easily be persuaded into giving Mr. Pretty Brown Eyes a whole lot of loving. Plus, I still had them drinks up in me, so I wasn't feeling any pain.

*****

"Hey lady, come and take a ride with me!" He said, sounding all sexy with his deep voice.

"I don't think so. I don't know you well enough to get on the back of that bike." *He must think that I'm like these other chicks. He got the wrong one.*

"That's the point, how do you expect to get to know me? I promise not to kill you!" He laughed.

"I looked back at Mika and of course she was egging me on. Talking about 'Go have some fun, girl.' So eventually, after some persuading, I hopped on the back of that bike and now my ass is wide open.

*****

We rode all over New Haven and I had a grip on him like no tomorrow. I could tell he worked out; his body was fit. I didn't notice all of this in the bar; all I was worried about was getting a free drink. We pulled up to Edgewood Park where it was nice and quiet just so we could talk. He picked me up and walked me over to this big rock and sat me down, staring at me with them eyes. I was praying to God that he didn't touch me in the wrong way because I wouldn't be able to control myself.

"So Liz, how come I never see you around? What, you don't come out?" He asked.

Damn, he remembers my name, and of course, I forgot his. "I go to work and come home. All I really care about is raising my kids and making sure that they're straight."

"How many kids do you have?" He asked, kind of nervous of my answer.

"Three girls," I replied.

"Oh," he sounded relieved. "You act like you got about five or six kids or something." He laughed. "You said you're single, why is that?"

"I've been through a thing or two, so I just haven't found anybody worthy of my time." *I'm not going to get into the whole Poncho fiasco.*

"You mean you haven't given anyone the time of day because you've been hurt a time or two. I'm very good at reading between the lines. Tell me I'm wrong." He smiled.

"I'm sorry, but what is your name? I forgot." I replied, trying to ignore his statement. *He was right on point.*

"Tyson. It should be in your phone. You've been riding around with me and didn't even know my name, shame on you Lizzy!" Tyson shook his head in a playful way. "Or maybe you did remember my name and just tried to change the subject. Am I right about what I said?"

"Maybe. So now it's my turn to ask the questions. Why are you single? How many kids do you have? How many baby mamas do you have? Do you have a job? Who do you live with? What do you want with me? Besides this bike, do you have a car?" *Yes honey, I have a lot of questions. I need to see if you're even worth me talking to.*

"Okay, slow down. You want my whole entire resume? I'll answer every single last question that you have. I'm single because women ain't shit! I have one son, that's twelve, that I have custody of, and we live in a townhouse by ourselves that I just purchased three years ago. I'm an electrician and have been for the last ten years. Not only do I have this bike, I also own a car and a truck. I don't know what I want with you yet. I like what I see on the outside, but I can't be sure until I see what you're like on the inside. Is that okay with you?" He asked.

"Very impressive. How long have you been single?" *That was nice, but I still have a few more questions for him.*

"I've been single for about year. I had sex last week, on a humble. I get approached by females on a regular, so if I feel like it, I might take them out here and there. I have nothing serious going on. I like to be very upfront so that there's no mistake in the communication." He said, being very direct.

"How was that sex you had last week?" I questioned.

"It was good, can't complain. I'm guessing you haven't had any in a while since you haven't opened yourself up; I don't know though, I could be wrong." Tyson said, not even budging; looking me straight in the eyes.

"It's been a long while." *I love this conversation. He seems to be so open and honest.* "What do you plan on doing with the person that you just had that good sex with?"

"Nothing at all. I enjoyed myself, she enjoyed herself and that's it. We're both grown. If we hook up again, then that's fine. If not, then that's okay too." Tyson shrugged his shoulders.

"Is that what you're looking for? Just a good time and so be it! You did say that women ain't shit!" *I need to know because I'm not looking for a one-night stand. I waited all this time and I'm not just going to give it to somebody just because.*

"Right now I'm going with the flow. Would I like to be in a relationship? The answer would be 'yes,' with the right person. I'm not out here looking for my soul mate, but if she happens to cross my path then I will welcome it. Are you hungry Miss Liz? I would like to continue this conversation at one of my favorite diners."

"Yes, I could stand to eat something to dry up some of this liquor in my system." I laughed.

*****

We hopped back on the bike and went to the diner to eat. We talked until five that morning, and finally he dropped me back off to my car, which I left at the bar. Me and Mika drove separately, just in case I wanted to leave early I could, so it all worked out. He thanked me for the lovely conversation, kissed me on hand and waited until I pulled off before he sped off on his bike. Then he called me to make sure I made it home safely and I haven't slept much since.

All I can think about is him now is I feel like a scared little teenager. All I've ever known was Poncho; he was my first and only. I've never been with anyone else, and I definitely don't ever remember me and Poncho being able to talk like this for hours on an intimate level. All our talks turned into arguments over him cheating. *There's something so special about Tyson that has me mesmerized.* I have to snap out of this. My girls are coming home today after being away from me all weekend, which didn't happen too often.

Now here goes Wanda interrupting my thoughts. She had been calling me all weekend, but I just ignored all her calls.

*****

"What's up Wanda?" *I'm not really in the mood.*

"Girl, I heard you was out and about. What was that all about?" Wanda asked with her nosey self. *I hope I'm not the hot topic of the week in New Haven.*

"Yep, I was out and had a very good time. That's what you're calling me for?" I'm trying to keep it short and sweet. *If she doesn't mention Tyson then neither am I.* Wanda has a bad habit of calling around to dig up dirt from twenty years ago and report it back. If there's anything I need to know I'm willing to take my chances and find out on my own without any pre-judgment.

"Girl no, have you talked to Poncho since he's been back?" Wanda asked.

"No Wanda, I haven't. I hardly ever talk to him anyway. What's up?" *I hate when she beats around the bush. Just get to the point.*

"Well brace yourself for this karma; word on the street is Chris ain't doing too good. Home-girl has locked herself in the house and won't come out. She hasn't been to work since she found out. I heard she might be a little suicidal. This thing with Poncho has torn her the hell up!" Wanda chuckled like it was funny. "Poor thing, he got her real good!"

"Wanda, I wish I could sit on this phone and tell you that I'm happy that she's hurting like this, but I can't. Had I not gotten out of that situation, I could very well be her. I feel bad for her because I understand where her state of mind is at right now!" *I know this is not the answer Wanda expected me to give her, but honestly, I'm just over the whole thing with Poncho. It doesn't even bother me anymore.*

"Oh no, she's getting everything that she deserves. She ran around behind your back with Poncho for years, and you want to play the sympathy card for her! Now she has to eat that pain. It was all-good when she was doing it to you! I remember her bragging talking about 'Yeah, I have her man, so what!'" Wanda was trying her best to get me hyped, as if I had forgotten.

"Poncho ran just as much game on her as he did me. She just lingered around longer than the others because I couldn't shake her. The others got shook and decided he wasn't worth it. If I go around being angry at every woman that he slept with, then I'll never be happy. The list is too long and the women were endless. I see that the cycle is still continuing on!" *Not today Wanda. You will not damper my spirits.* "I'm so glad my brain unfroze and my heart couldn't take any more of him and his shit! When I think of Poncho, I just want to throw up!"

"I hear you; did you tell the girls that they have a step-mother?" Wanda asked.

"Nope, that's for him to do. I'm sure they will be meeting her soon, whenever he decides to get them again. It's not my place to tell them anything. For all I know, he might not want them to know. The only reason why I know is because of you. I'm probably going to play stupid and act like I still don't know, until he tells me." *I'm not giving Wanda too much to run with today. I know what to say and what not to say to her. The Wanda News Channels travels faster than any plane.*

"If I was you, I would give my girls a heads up. They're going to be looking for Chris and their little brother. Stuff like this can shock a kid!" Wanda said, as if she was concerned about my girls' well-being.

"Well you're not me, and I think I know how to handle my girls. They know how to come to me with any issues that they have." I said, rolling my eyes.

"Okay girl, no need to get so snappy! I'm just trying to look out for you." Wanda said on the defense.

"Let me go so I can start my dinner. I will talk to you later."

*****

I hung up the phone with the intentions on making dinner, but something said to get in my car and drive over to check on Chris, and before you know it, I was knocking on her door. She wasn't answering and the nosey neighbors were peeping out the doors and windows. My guess is that I wasn't the only one trying to get her to come to the door.

"Chris it's me, Liz! I know you're in there, please open the door!" I was yelling and pleading.

Slowly but surely Chris unlocked the door and allowed me to push my way in. Her apartment was covered in shattered glass. I had to watch my step so I didn't cut my foot. *She must have been in here breaking shit up.* She looked a hot mess, hair all over the place, bags under her eyes; she was just lying there on the couch.

I could tell she must have taken some food out that she never cooked or put away, because it smelled like spoiled meat. I had to hold my breath in, as my OCD kicked in. I walked into the kitchen and sure enough, a bag of chicken was sitting in the sink. I quickly put it in the trash, opened up the window, and took a quick glance over at her as I walked over to the dumpster to get rid of the trash. I made my way back in, grabbed the broom and immediately started sweeping up the glass. Chris didn't utter one word. There was nothing but dead silence as she lay in that same spot, looking like a dead corpse. Once I finished sweeping, I sat on the loveseat directly across from her.

*****

"Chris, you can't do this. You have a son that needs his mother. You have a job to go to and bills that need to be paid. There is life outside of Poncho; how do I know? Just look at me! You want to lay here and just die! I understand, but guess what? While you're wallowing in self-pity Poncho is still married, living his life! Do you think he's missing a beat? Get your ass up and get yourself together!" I yelled slightly.

Nothing but dead silence. All she did was roll over with her back to me.

"Chris, how long have you been lying on that couch? Where is your son? Turn around and look at me!" I yelled. She listened. "Sit up!" *Yelling seems to be working for me.* "This man doesn't have a job, can't do shit for you, but give you a wet ass; and you think he's worthy of all of this!" I looked around her apartment. "He's a whore, and you're letting a whore win! Does he pay your bills? Your son is in a daycare and his father doesn't work! Does he cook your food? Does he run your bath water and wipe your ass?"

"NO, NO, NO, STOP IT!" Chris yelled. *I finally got a reaction out of her.*

"No, you stop it!" I yelled back. "You're about to lose everything over community dick!"

"You don't understand, he married her, put our son in the wedding. I helped him pay for that wedding, and I wasn't even the bride! How could I be so stupid? It's dark in here because they came and turned off my lights because I thought I was saving him from going to jail! I didn't pay my bills for a nigga that was marrying the next bitch!" Chris was crying uncontrollably.

Oh my God! I want to cry for her. Lord, please give me the right words to say. I had no idea that he put their son in the wedding. Oh, Wanda was slipping; she left out a major detail to Poncho and his madness.

"Chris, listen to me." I walked over to the couch, sat down next to her and wrapped my arms around her. "This too shall pass. When we're in love with a man a whole lot of things fly over our heads. We've all played the fool for love at least once in our lives. This pain that you're feeling will let up; it just takes time. He will get his in due time. You need to find your self-worth, and we're going to bring back your self-esteem."

"How did you do it? How did you get over him? I can't even say his name; it hurts too much!" Chris asked, still crying her eyes out.

"I realized that I was chasing a dream. He wasn't shit and was never going to be shit! I knew I wasn't losing a damn thing, but had everything to gain by getting rid of him. So I let you have him! I lost myself in Poncho. I woke up one day and asked myself, 'What is wrong with me?' I didn't like the woman that I became, and I wanted better for me and my girls. I don't want you to ever think that I left Poncho because of you. I left Poncho alone for me! I allowed a man to control my every being; my life was no longer my life, it was his. I wanted me back! There was no way that I could have loved me when I was letting a man run all over me. The day I put him out I could feel the weight being lifted. It was sooo heavy! I took full responsibility and stopped blaming you and all the other women, because at the end of the day, y'all didn't break my heart, he did!" My heart was breaking for Chris. I allowed Poncho to cause me a lot of unnecessary pain and that's what I need for Chris to realize.

"I played my part and I apologize to you. I know I'm a day late and dollar too short." Chris tried to smile through her tears. "What made you come over here? I never expected you in a million years!"

"Funny how life is. I didn't expect me to either. Wanda called with her gossip and told me how she was told that you were suicidal. I remember the days and nights that I wanted to die just so I wouldn't have to feel the pain. So who better to come over here, other than me?" For once Wanda running off at her mouth caused a good deed.

"Thank you for coming. When I heard your voice at the door I didn't know what to expect. All kind of thoughts went through my head. I never expected you to reach out to me with help. I just knew you were here to make me feel worse. This is really big of you; you sound like you're sincere, because I don't want your pity!" Chris was still crying.

"I could be doing a million other things right now. I'm here because you need me to be. I'm the only one that knows what you're going through. This has nothing to do with pity. I'm not holding any grudges towards you at all. I have no intentions on running out of here causing you any ill will. We may not be friends, but we both are women that got caught up in the same bad ass spell of Poncho! Now, if you want me to leave, then I have no problem doing so, but we both know that's not what you want! You opened that door for a reason!" *I'm not about to sit here and try and convince Chris that I'm not out to get her. Me being here should be more than enough. The average chick would be somewhere celebrating her pain.*

"I'm sorry. It's just hard to believe, that's all. At one point we couldn't even see each other without fighting. Oh Liz, he made me feel so worthless. I really just want to hurt him sooo bad!" Chris balled up her fist.

"You can hurt him, by getting yourself together and putting a smile on your face. Right now the loser is winning." *I know it's easier said than done, but Chris has to pull herself together.*

"I feel like I lost, even though I hear everything you're saying. This is going to be hard for me!" Chris said, while taking the tissue that I gave her from out the bathroom to wipe her tears. I just took the whole roll out; she needs it. Her eyes are bloodshot red and swollen from crying so much.

"It was hard for me. Poncho was my first love. Healing is a process that doesn't happen overnight. Unfortunately, the process isn't easy either. Even though I was tired of him and wanted him out, it still hurt me. I suffered horribly while I was in the relationship, so I always just reverted back to that, and that's what got me through. I will tell you this; laying here on this couch, keeping your mind idle, is not helping at all." The worst thing you can do during a break-up is sit still. Once I started moving around and keeping myself busy, little by little the less I thought about what I was going through.

"I can't function; I don't know what else to do! I can't go to work, I'm too sick. I can't take care of my son properly because my mind is not stable! I don't want to be seen. I feel like the biggest dummy alive. I just want to hide until I can be strong enough to deal with everything that transpired. My emotions are all over the place; I'm just stuck!" Chris said, lying back down on the couch, grabbing her blanket.

"Chris, you have to change your mindset and start speaking strength into yourself. You have to keep saying, 'He's not worth my sanity, my peace of mind', and you call him every name that you can think of every day until your pain subsides! You have to tell yourself, 'I'm better than this,' even if you don't believe it. The more you say it, eventually you will start to believe it yourself! This is not all about you, Chris; your son needs you." *I have to keep it cool since she's in a fragile state. I don't want her to take things the wrong way.* "Get you some clothes, you're coming home with me, and then we can figure out how we're going to get these lights back on."

"Thank you, but I can just go over to my Mom's; she has my son. You've already went out of your way by coming over here."

"Nope, we can pick him up on the way so he can spend time with his sisters. I'm cooking a nice little dinner tonight; you need to eat! I won't take no for an answer. Let's go!" I demanded. I've seen her mother in action and being over there is not going to help Chris.

"Okay. Let me grab some clothes!" Chris managed to get off that couch and make her way into the bedrooms.

"Yes, because you're getting in the shower too." Not that I smelled her, but she looked like she hadn't taken a shower or bath either.

CHAPTER 10

THE BUM SQUAD

PONCHO

𝒪'm just sitting here waiting for my boys to arrive. Wifey got me a nice little set up in the basement. Pool table, a fully stocked bar, sixty inch flat screen hanging on the wall, chocolate leather sectional, accented in off white, with a bunch of throw pillows. *Lisa really knows how to treat me. I wish they would hurry up. I'm anxious to show off my come up. Of course Rich is the first to arrive. I hope he ain't coming over here whining about his wife. I'm not in the mood to even hear the shit.*

*****

"What's up?" I greet him at the door before he could ring the doorbell.

"It ain't nothing man." Rich stared around at the yard. Lisa keeps everything in tact; we have a landscaper that comes out weekly. "Damn this is nice out here, I like."

"Yeah, I'm happy living out here in Woodbridge. It's peaceful and can't too many people find me out here. Come on in. Let's go down to my man cave and play a game of pool while we wait for the niggas that's on CP time!"

*****

Rich followed me down to the basement. He was looking around in amazement.

"Man, Poncho, what does your wife do for a living?" Rich asked.

"She's a CEO for Mack & Taylor. I guess she makes a pretty good living for us. No complain'ts over here."

"I guess not. Getting with her was like hitting the *Mega Millions*. I see why you married her now. I can't remember…does she have any sisters?" Rich laughed as he was picking up the pool stick.

"Nope, only girl…spoiled rotten. Always lived the good life. You want a beer or something?" I asked.

"Yeah, I'll take a beer. I thought Lisa was a church girl?" Rich asked with a puzzled look. Just because Lisa is saved does not mean I am. She knows that I drink and every now and then she'll have a glass of wine.

"Yeah she is, she just knows what I like." I handed Rich his beer.

"Are you starting to love her?" Rich took a sip of his beer knowing damn well that I don't love anybody. I care about women; that's just how my mind is set up.

"I like her a lot; she really knows how to cater to a man. She's different from any woman that I've ever been with. There isn't anything that she wouldn't do for me. She's real laid back; there's this calmness to her. I can't really explain it, but you get where I'm going with this!"

"Yeah, I kind of understand what you're trying to say. Where's she at now?" Rich asked.

"She's out handling some family business with her cousin. She'll be gone for a while, so that's why it was perfect timing to have the fellas come over, sit back, have a few drinks and laughs. Get away from the Ave. for a little bit. Now we can come here sometimes and chill." It's been years since one of us could actually offer a chill spot to one another. Dominique wasn't having us all up in her house. It just so happens, that Lisa doesn't mind. She would rather have me home more, and this right here will do it. I'm still going to be in the streets, just not as much as I used to.

"That's what's up! I don't really know her like that, but she seems like she's cool people. What's up with Chris? I heard she wasn't doing too well. Have you spoken to her?" Rich asked. His concern for Chris was genuine. I guess you could say that was his girl. Rich really liked her for me and wanted us to be together. Out of all the chicks that I've ever been with, my boys always said that Chris was the coolest. She looked out for any one of them. Her motto was, 'Any friend of mine was a friend of hers.'

"I don't really know, I haven't really reached out yet. I'm giving her time to calm down a little bit. Man she went sick on me over a piece of paper. Do you believe that shit? She came off like she never knew what was good. Yeah I was there with her, but she knew it wasn't all about her! Chris knew that I was out here doing my thang. I guess the whole marriage thing threw her for a loop. All she had to do is rock with me. I was gonna make sure her and my son would be okay, but no, she wanted to try and get stupid! I can't understand these bitches!" *Women are something else.*

"You can't really blame her; you planned a whole wedding while still living with her! Poncho, that girl loved you. You should be looking at it like, 'What if the shoe was on the other foot?'" Rich asked.

"I would have to accept it. Not saying that I would like it, but it is what it is. I'm not going to go crazy and lose my mind behind a piece a pussy. I damn sure wouldn't shed a tear. Whatever makes her happy then that's just that! I keep trying to tell y'all that I think different from the average man out here." I never wear my feelings on my sleeve. Now I've seen Rich in action even before he married Dominique. He would be messing with a chick on the side and get mad at the side chick for messing around on him. Knowing good and well he can't put that kind of time in because of his main chick. I'm not selfish like that, if Honesty needs to handle her business before I get back around to her, then that's her right. Now my wife is a different story, she doesn't have an excuse. One, because she doesn't know my dirt, and I hope it stays that way. Two, because she gets my time. Whenever she calls I immediately drop everything and do whatever she asks.

"Let Dominique try some crazy mess like that. I'm going off! Off to the point where I will be back in jail! There won't be no happily ever after. Six feet under that dirt is where he and she will go!" Rich was serious as hell. *He got some nerve. This fool must have forgotten that he was the one that ruined his marriage. He expects Dominique to always live in his shadow, not going to happen, bro. I hope that little college chick that he's living with makes him fall in love.* From what I've been hearing, Dominique has already moved on with her life. She's supposed to be messing with some dude that works with her at Yale. For all he knows that could have been going on. I'm just going to hold on tight to that little word on the street. If he ever hears about it, it didn't come from me.

*****

We heard Quan's loud ass car pull up. *I wish he would just get the muffler fixed to quiet that car down.* You can hear him coming before he even turns the corner. I ran upstairs to greet him, a nice little distraction to change the subject.

*****

"Hey man, you really made it to the big time!" Quan yelled as he was walking up to the house with a forty of Old English in his hand. *This isn't the neighborhood for his Ghetto ass.* "This is like some shit you see in a magazine!"

I laughed. Quan is always over the top and he's the one that came from something, the rest of us didn't. "Follow me to the basement. This is my man cave, where I spend most of my time when I'm in the house." Poncho said. "Rich is already down there chilling."

"Yeah, I saw his car out there when I pulled up. He would be the first one here. Damn, you hit the jackpot with this one." Quan stopped in his tracks to take a brief look at some of the house that his eyes could see. *When Mickey and Trey get here, that's when I will give them a full tour. I want to get it done and over with in one shot.* "Don't mess this up Poncho!" Quan said, bopping down the stairs.

*****

"What up, Richy Rich? What's going on my brother?" Quan gave Rich dap.

"Shit, I can't call it! Getting ready to embrace this pool table, you down to get your ass whooped?" Rich laughed.

"I see you're still on your competitive bullshit! Go ahead and break so I can send you home crying!" Quan said while pouring him a shot of Hennessy.

While Rich and Quan were going at it playing pool, Mickey and Trey arrived. *Good, just in time to instigate and irritate the hell out of Rich and Quan, egging them on making side bets as to which one would win the game. Now the real fun begins, just us fellas drinking and talking shit like old times. I'm staying out of it like I do, sitting back watching them have fun. Rich won the first game and Quan won the second, so before they get to the grand finale I want to give them a full tour of the house.*

*****

"Come on fellas; let me show y'all the rest of the house." Yeah, they were anxious to see. Everything came to a cease as they all followed me back up the stairs. I'm smiling the whole time in my head but keeping my cool. *I can't let them see how excited I am so I'm playing it cool acting all nonchalant.* All I hear is, 'Damn son,' 'Damn man,' 'This is the shit,' the whole time I'm walking them through.

I saved the master bedroom for last, this room had a mind of its own, a masterpiece in itself. Jacuzzi, his and her bathroom, balcony, and a sitting area with a couch; to be honest the master bedroom was bigger than some people's one bedroom apartment. Talk about impressed; they couldn't believe it.

*****

We made our way back down to my man cave and we all took a celebration shot. *Since we were getting tipsy I figure let me hit Honesty up. I'm a little overdue for my frequent visits, but she didn't hit me back yet. The fellas are getting a bit happy with that*

Hennessey bottle. *I don't mind them drinking it up, but I mind them driving out here in Woodbridge. I need to make sure they get home safely, so I'm wrapping this thing up.*

*****

"Okay y'all, wifey should be coming home soon." As I look at my watch it's only eight o'clock, the night is still early. *She probably won't be home for another hour or so, but still it's a good excuse to get them out of here.*

"Alright man, we know what that means, that's our cue to get the hell out of here!" Quan started blowing kisses. "I'm going to miss your house!" *I might be a little too late; Quan is definitely drunk. Oh yeah, he was drinking before he got here.*

"One of y'all need to drop him off. I'll come get him in the morning so he can take that loud ass car home, but he's not driving from here. The Po Po doesn't have anything better to do out here!" I laughed.

"Yeah, I got him," Rich said. See you later Poncho, The Man, thanks for inviting us up, appreciate it bro. I know I needed this escape."

"Shoot, we all did!" Trey said. "Yeah, thank you man!"

I watched as they all pulled off, checking my phone to see if Honesty hit me back; still no reply. *I guess I'll just chill for the night.*

CHAPTER 11

LIZ

Chris ended up spending a whole week with me until we managed to get her lights cut back on. We reached out to a couple of churches that helped, and she qualified for some energy assistance. Our week together was pretty cool. My girls were happy to be spending time with their little brother.

Chris and I bonded together like we were never enemies. She went back to work, of course, not without getting written up, which was very much understandable. She was put on a ninety-day probation that consisted of; she couldn't be late or miss any days. I had to remind her every day to just give her an extra push to get out of her feelings and be about her business. It was cool though, having someone to help out with the girls and I helped her out with her son.

We each took turns dropping off and picking up, which gave us some extra time in the mornings. We rotated cooking dinner every night. For the most part, Chris was pretty busy and it kept her mind off of Poncho, but she was still having her breakdowns with plenty more to come. He did her dirty, so it was going to take her a long time to get over him, but like I told her, I'm going to be right here coaching her all the way through her pain.

I went out a couple of times with Tyson while she watched the kids. We worked well together as a team, true sisterhood. When she went home she had an eviction notice waiting for her. She was behind in her rent, just another hurdle for her to cross. She cried and cried. All I could do was listen and give her words of encouragement. Getting ready to lose your place behind a no good man who really could care less. Shame on her, but I can't be the one to pass judgement because the same thing happened to me with the same damn man. *I hope his wife has more sense than we had because if she doesn't see this train wreck coming, God help her!* The two lessons that I learned from Poncho are to go to work and pay my bills, no matter what I'm going through. All I was doing was bringing on more problems to my life that didn't have to be there had I put me first.

Tyson was ringing my phone. Every time he calls my face lights up like a kid in a candy store.

*****

"Hello there!" I answered sounding very seductive.

"What's up?" Tyson asked.

"Nothing, just laying here. Was getting ready to take it down." I replied.

"Already, it's only nine o'clock on a Friday night!" Tyson laughed. "You're such an old lady."

"I know, I know! Once the girls go to sleep I don't really have much to do, so I just follow suit." *I'm wide-awake now baby. Only for you, at least that's what my mind is saying.*

"I must change that because I can think of quite a few things that you could be doing right now." Tyson said.

"Oh yeah, I'm afraid to ask what those things consist of!" I laughed knowing very well what Tyson was talking about. He wants my goodies, and Lord knows I sure want every bit of him, but I'm going to hold out a little bit longer. The last thing I need him believing is that I'm easy. *Oh no brother, you will wait.*

"Well you're grown and an intelligent lady, I'm sure that you can figure it out. So what are your plans for the rest of the weekend?" Tyson asked as if he already made plans for me.

"I'm not sure. I don't have anything special planned, just the usual laundry, grocery shopping, cleaning." I'm secretly hoping that he wants to do something with me this weekend.

"Can a brother wine and dine you on Saturday? Do I have to pay for a babysitter?" *Now Tyson was turning me on even more.*

"I'm sure I can find a babysitter, where are you taking me?" I asked out of curiosity.

"It's a surprise. I can pick you up around three. Make sure you have a babysitter for the whole night." *He ain't saying nothing but a word. I love to be surprised. I'm more than ready.*

"Okay, I will see you tomorrow at three." I said grinning from the ear to ear.

*****

I hung up the phone on cloud nine. *Now I have to figure out who is going to watch the girls. What the hell am I going to wear? Thank goodness I have a fresh weave; I guess I will rod this hair up.* Since I don't go out much, I definitely have to hit the stores tomorrow to find me a nice dress. He said for the whole night, he must plan on getting some from me. *Oh my God!* Physically I'm ready, but mentally I wonder. Just as I finished putting my last rod in my hair Mika was calling me. This had to be important because she knows I'm usually sleeping by now.

*****

"Hello" I answered.

"Girl, there's some chick outside my building looking for Rich, threatening to whoop my ass! She's screaming from the top of her lungs! I just called the cops!" Mika sounded shook.

"Where the hell is he?" I asked pissed off. *This was not cool to have some chick outside my girl's apartment. She's lucky I have these kids or else I would be over there.*

"I called him; he claims he's on his way! He has got to go, she's out here with an infant and two toddlers talking about Rich better come home to his family! I have no time for this. Now she's throwing shit up at my window. She is out here putting on a show. What kind of woman brings an infant with her to fight? These cops are taking too long!" Mika said anxiously.

"Oh yes, get rid of him now, matter of fact, pack his shit up now! I'm staying on this phone with you until the police get there!" *I wonder what's taking the NHPD so long. They can't be playing around with this domestic shit. Too many people are getting hurt these days. I told Mika about being so gullible when it comes down to these men. Now maybe she will use some caution and listen.*

"Girl, I'll call you back, Rich just pulled up with my car!" Mika said sounding relieved.

"I'll be waiting!" *Now I'm going to be up half the night worried about Mika. I'm tempted to call Chris and see if she's up so she can come over here while I go check on Mika. Nope, I'm leaving Chris alone. She has enough going on than to be taking on my friends' problems; then again, it might not be such a bad idea. I know for a fact listening to Mika helped me see even more.*

CHAPTER 12

THE BUM SQUAD

PONCHO

𝓘'm just chilling on the Ave. flexing in my new gray BMW 740 that wifey bought me waiting on the fellas to arrive, which was our daily routine, jumping in and out acting like I was looking at my tires. I wanted the whole New Haven to see what I was driving. *Wait until my squad sees this shit. Now this is my kind of living.*

I can't wait to see Honesty a little later. We've been hanging ever since I met her that day. I like her, she's low main'tenance; we hook up when I can, and she gives me no problems at all. All women need to take a page out of her book. I can disappear and then hit her up, she don't even ask me questions. She doesn't care where I've been or what I've been doing. Our time is just our time.

Recently I tried reaching out to Chris, but I guess she has me on the block list because the phone goes straight to voice mail. I thought that maybe she would answer for Quan's phone, but she didn't answer the call from his phone either, but it's cool. I'm going to give her a little more time before I move on to the next.

I always roll with three women or more. Right now I'm down to two and that ain't cutting it. I have room for one or two more.

Wifey be gone a lot running that company, handling family obligations, so all I have is time on my hands. I like it that way. I can't have somebody smothering me to death blowing up my spot and slowing down my flow.

Here in New Haven, with a shortage of men, we can basically do what we want to do. Women will take what they can get. Back in the day the women had it their way, but I like how times have changed. It's really a man's world and I'm enjoying every bit of it. I wish my boys would wake up and jump on the bandwagon so they can stop letting these women run them. The only one that I think gets it is Quan.

*****

"Hey man it's about time." Mickey had to do a double take. *Yeah I like that.*

"What, what, who's ride you in?" Mickey walked around my BMW admiring the hell out of it.

"Mine nigga! Wifey got it for me!" I said smiling from ear to ear.

"Damn man, I'm trying to be like you! What I got to do?" Mickey asked. "First the house, now this!" Mickey pointed at my car.

"Stop messing with them chicken heads and get you a real bitch, it's a simple solution. Get up out them projects, son! Jump in so you can get the full effect!" Mickey jumped in the passenger side and shut the door like we was running from the police or something. I wanted to laugh, but I kept my composure.

"This is nice man, I can't even lie!" Mickey said while staring at the dashboard. "Let me find her and I will lick her ass...now that's something I don't do! I'm dead ass serious!"

I couldn't help but to laugh at this amused fool. "Why are you late anyway?"

"I had to drop China off at work. The bus was running late!" Mickey said.

"I know that's Melinda's car you driving. So now you and China back on good terms again?" I asked being curious; not that this was nothing new. Mickey been going in between those two women for the longest.

"Yeah, we good for now. China missed the bus this morning and hit me up for a ride. After I dropped off Melinda I went and picked her up and dropped her off too. Now I have to hear Melinda's mouth about gas. She filled up the tank and said that it has to last her for the week. I can't be out here joy riding this week." Mickey sounded as if it was the end of the world.

"Man, you should have asked China for some gas money or got that bus fare! Shiittt, you stupid; always trying to play Mr. Nice Guy, fuck that!" *When will they learn to train these women? I'm right here setting the stage and they still can't follow. Only my squad. I would have been able to fill the tank up three times. I wish a woman would tell me that I can't be riding around! These niggas are in the wrong damn game.*

"You right, I should have got that bus fare! I wasn't thinking, but I'll hit her up on Friday, when it's payday. She'll look out for me!" Mickey said.

"Yeah right, what you gonna get, twenty dollars? You better learn how to start stacking them hundreds." Good thing I saw Rich looking around for us, so I beeped the horn and waved my hand for him to come over here. I was ready to end this stupid conversation.

*****

"Get in!" Rich jumped right in the back seat.

"So this is how we rolling today? I hear that shit! Who you been tricking with that got you this rental? Rich asked.

"Naw, this is how we rolling every day! Say Hello to Miss Grey!" I said being cocky, bopping my head. *Yeah look at me!* "Wifey got me this. She said I needed an upgrade from the Honda. Plus, she couldn't stand the fact that Lucinda bought it for me. I tried to tell her that home girl is happily married these days and ain't even thinking about me! She wants us to have new beginnings so she took me on the lot and this is what I grabbed." I said putting my hands on the dashboard.

"Damn Son, wifey making moves like this, I guess she will be around for a while! She making it hard for you to pull out from underneath the rug! " Rich laughed. *As if material shit has ever stopped me. I'm going to do what I want to do.*

"Since when have you known me to stop doing me?" I had to remind Rich of who he was talking to. *I'm Poncho all day, everyday...no matter what.*

"Yo, Quan, we over here!" Rich yelled from the back seat. I didn't even see my boy Quan roll up! I was too busy running my mouth.

*****

Trey was the only one missing out. He was on babysitting duty as usual. I blasted the music while we went cruising the streets early in the morning rocking to Biggie like it was a Friday night. I think we might have hit every main and side-street there was in New Haven. We had the windows down, sunroof open, bopping our heads to the music. It felt like we were back in the day when Quan had all that money.

After a while, I got tired of them, and went and scooped up Honesty. Fucked their whole groove up, which I already knew it would. It wasn't much longer before the Bum Squad started asking to be dropped off back on the Ave. That's exactly what I wanted to hear so I could get some quality time with my number two lady!

I took Honesty to the house since wifey was at work. I showed her around my man cave, told her to relax and get comfortable on the couch; turned on the T.V. for her while I went upstairs in the kitchen to make us something quick to eat. I was hungry and so was she.

I decided on a big late breakfast since it was early afternoon. I made some grilled cheese, scrambled eggs, bacon, and sausage, cut up some cantaloupe, and poured two glasses of orange juice. I put our plates on a tray and carried them downstairs. Impressed she was. She said I didn't look like the type to cook. I don't know what the cooking type looks like, but a brother can cook. I used to watch my sisters cook up some heavy meals, so I learned a thing or two.

We ate our food; I knocked those boots on the couch. I wasn't bringing her in the bedroom; I would have to change the sheets. This way all I had to do was take a rag and wipe down the couch. Yep, I took the lazy way out!

Honesty fell asleep on top of me, butt naked and I dozed off as well. We woke up around four, which was perfect timing. I wasn't sure if wifey was getting off at five or staying late. She usually didn't give me a heads up. We put our clothes on and I dropped off my Boo, until the next time.

CHAPTER 13

KEISHA

All three of my babies got taken away from me when I got locked up. DCF (Department of Children and Families) considered me to be unfit since I had the children with me while I was outside beating Rich with that dog chain. He wanted to be a dog, so I was determined he would get treated like one. He was trying to run from me, but the chain was so long that it was impossible. I gave him a chance to bring his ass home with me but when he didn't, and decided that he was going to deny our children for some lame ass chick that he just met and decided to play house with. I kind of lost it. Now my babies are caught up in the system, separated in foster homes. The least they could have done was kept them together. I have so many charges pending against me that it don't make any sense, and this fool was cooperating with the prosecutors. You would think that since I have his babies he wouldn't be trying to make these charges stick, but he was.

He's a sorry motherfucker, but I love him. He was given the chance to take all three of the kids but the social worker told me he said that he couldn't do it. He's so full of shit. He could have helped, Rich just didn't want to.

I damn near asked every family member that I thought would be capable of getting my kids in their custody, except Dominique, and they all turned me down. All they had to do was get them and I would resume my position and handle my responsibilities. I hit every dead end that you can possibly think of, but they don't have to worry about me no more. As far as I'm concerned, I don't have any family!

My mother did bail me out, but that was it. She said I was on my own from now on. All she was worried about was that I show up for court, fearing that her raggedy house would get taken. I was surprised she even did that, so I guess I should be grateful.

My face was plastered all over the New Haven news stations and I made the front page of the New Haven Register. The news made me out to be the worst mother ever. That's what you get when you live in small ass New Haven; any news is news. Anybody that knows me knows that I love my kids. The only place they go without me is to daycare and that's it. Daycare was the only break that I got from my children, and I had to do that by beating the system.

Social Services had me in this work program that I never went to a day in my life. It pays to have a little connection to sign me in and out. All I did was go looking for my man, just like any other woman would have done.

It was almost a month too long of me not seeing Rich and him avoiding me. I told Wanda to find out where that bitch lived at and she delivered the info that I requested. Enough was enough. He never even saw our new baby until that night. Ricka was almost four weeks old. What pissed me off the most was when he did that little smirk and frowned up his face when he saw her. *Chris was right, I should have just kept my mouth shut and not told Dominique. A piece of him was better than nothing at all.* I could have handled it much different without him finding out that my hands were even in the mix.

Now I have to figure out a way to get Rich back into my life. *Maybe if I try and kill myself he will come rushing to my bedside. That's going to be my last resort!* I'm pretty sure I scared off old weakness. That bitch ran her ass back in that apartment so quick and was looking from a distance. She didn't even have his back, but I guess that's what he likes these days, young, weak bitches! If the tables were turned, Rich and I would have been out there double-teaming, eventually one of us would have grabbed ahold of that dog chain. As mad as I am right now, let a bitch touch him and see what I do!

*****

I wish I knew what happened to Rich; he was my friend before anything even happened between us. Back when he was hustling I would just be sitting on my porch late night while he was handling his business all up and down Winchester Ave. Every night, like clockwork, somewhere around eleven, he would just walk on by me while I would be sitting on my mother's porch. One night he stumbled on my mother's porch with me. I remember that day is as if it were today.

He was high out of his mind mumbling, "Why you always out here on this porch like this at night? Rain, snow, or shine, you're always out here! You need to be in the house sleeping!" I laughed because I thought he was funny. Why was he so concerned about me? I didn't even know that he saw me out here night after night. From that night on, we were cool. As he would be making his rounds, I would prepare him a nice plate of whatever me and my mother cooked. He would sit out on the porch with me, eat his food, and we would talk mostly about what went down on the Ave. earlier that day. Then one night he got drunk, I wasn't letting him drive home like that. Being the good friend that I was, I snuck him in my bedroom and used that as invitation to show Rich exactly what he was sleeping on. Later on that morning when he woke up he was a little startled. I must have turned him out because he kept coming back for some more of me. I knew he had a girl, he never hid that from me, but I never thought he loved her. How could he love her when he was fucking me?

CHAPTER 14

LIZ

Tyson surprised me and took me to New York; he sure knew how to woo a lady. I had no idea where we were going or what the itinerary was. He didn't even let me know how I should dress, so I ran out early that morning; went to TJ Maxx to find me a little dress to put on, not too dressy and not too casual.

I wanted to be sexy but comfortable, so I found me this cute little money-green dress that complimented my petite shape, showing just a tad bit a cleavage. I ran over in the shoe department and found me some nice brown wedge sandals to go with my brown pocketbook that I already had hanging in the closet. I had plenty of other accessories that would dress my outfit up the way I wanted it. I only spent forty dollars, staying within my budget. I've never been a label whore. I buy what my money allows me to, and look just as good as the next chick that spent hundreds, and she still might not look as good as me.

When he picked me up, he got out the car and rang the doorbell, no just beeping the horn and waiting for me to come out. He didn't even call and tell me he was on his way. I opened up the door and he said, "Damn you look nice." I said thank you as I was shutting the door behind me. I guess I could have invited him in, but I was anxious to see where he was taking me. I let him know that he didn't look too bad himself. I'm glad I did decide on that dress because he had on a pair of black slacks with a white button up shirt and some soft bottom black shoes, smelling all good. Beyond handsome he was. He opened up my door for me, like a real gentleman should. *Now this is the type of treatment that I can really get used to.*

We talked the whole ride. I had to fill him in on Mika and her drama from the night before; we both were tripping. As soon as I heard Rich pleading with her in the background I knew exactly what she was dealing with. Even after I gave her the 411 on everything that I knew, he still managed to talk his way into being kept. I'm a little disappointed in Mika for not listening to me once again. Cheating wasn't unusual for Rich, but I was in shock to find out that he had kids by Keisha. Ms. Gossip Queen, Wanda, didn't even let that one out of the bag, there's a reason why. She tells everything else. I'll have to ask Wanda about that the next time I talk to her.

Tyson told me that he was glad I didn't have a babysitter; he didn't want me over there involved in other people's problems and drama. His exact words were, "I realize that's your girl, but she's grown, and if she chooses to be stupid then you let her." Tyson is a no nonsense type of dude. I can see now that I'm going to have to chill on how much I tell him. He seems a little overprotective too. He said he don't want to have to hurt nobody. Tyson was serious; he didn't even crack a smile. I had to start talking about the kids just to change the subject to loosen him up a bit, and lucky for me it worked.

*****

When we got to Manhattan we checked into the Manhattan Hotel, where he had made reservations for us. *No wonder he told me to pack a bag and to make sure I had a babysitter.* The hotel was gorgeous, very upscale. It looked like one you would see in a movie. The location couldn't have been any better, right across from Times Square. *I really like Tyson's taste; he's a man with class.*

*****

We dropped our bags off in the room and headed back out. I only got to glance at the room we would be staying in, but I could tell it wasn't cheap. Well nothing is cheap in New York anyway. When we walked out, Tyson had a horse and buggy that took us all around Manhattan. Then we had dinner at the Roof Top as the sun was setting.

The food was delicious and the scenery was amazing. We could see everything; the lighting made it that much more romantic. All the couples, including ourselves, wanted our pictures taken, so we helped each other out by swapping phones and flicking it up. Then we went back to the hotel to end the night with some *Moscato* on ice. We ended up drinking the whole bottle. I was nice and tipsy. Tyson said he needed something stronger than that for him to be buzzing. He laughed at me.

Next thing I know, he undressed me butt ass naked, picked me up, and carried me into the Jacuzzi. He was so smooth and gentle with me. I guess that's what happens when you wear a dress; it doesn't take much to get that off. Then he undressed himself. Oh lord I couldn't watch. The shyness in me set in as I laid back and closed my eyes.

I felt him as he slid in right next to me. My heart was beating fast and my body was trembling. He started caressing my breasts and kissing me on my neck. I wanted to scream but I held my composure and moaned like never before. Lord knows it had been so long since I let a man touch me. I almost forgot how it felt.

He kissed me on my lips and said, "Open your eyes, I want to see you and I want you to see me."

I didn't want to, but I did. Thank goodness we were in the water and he couldn't feel what was going on between my legs. I was so wet that it felt like I was peeing on myself.

"Do you want me?" Tyson asked in his deep voice.

I mumbled, "Yes!"

He slid his tongue in my mouth and we started kissing, then he started caressing my sweet spot, as Poncho would say, and I had my first orgasm in over two years. He knew it too from the way that I screamed.

Tyson whispered in my ear, "Already, baby girl? I'm just getting started."

Then he slid over on top of me, lifted my ass up, and gently penetrated the hell out of me. He took his time with me, no rushing at all. I felt every single last stroke. It was like everything was happening in slow motion. He wanted us to cum together this time and that's exactly what happened. He picked me up and laid me on the bed while he went and grabbed a towel to dry me off. I couldn't stop my legs from shaking. My body was in a world of its own that even my mind couldn't control. I guess that was a turn on for him. Next thing I know we were back at it again, and again, and again.

Poncho doesn't have anything on Tyson's stroke. Poncho might be bigger in size, but he can never work a body over the way Tyson can. Tyson has me on a high that I never want to come down from.

I slept so good that I didn't even hear Tyson when he left or came back in with breakfast. He had to wake me up to eat. I'm usually a light sleeper, you can drop a pen and I'll wake up. I guess that's the mother instinct in me.

I wish we had more time in New York. I wasn't ready to come back, but I knew we had to. He had to get his son and I had to pick up my girls. I wanted to stay glued to him.

CHAPTER 15

CHRIS

"Chris, I raised you better than this. You out here making us look bad! Mopping around here for a no good ass nigga!" *I really don't feel like hearing my mother's mouth. I'm not in the mood for this shit. I only came over here to celebrate my sister's birthday and that's all I want to do.*

"Mom, I'm not in this mood for this. All I want to do is take my mind off of everything and have a good time with my family! Can you at least let me do that?" I asked.

"See child, this is why I tried to spare you from pain. No man will come in my house and take a shower or drink a glass of water if he ain't paying the water bill! No man will come in my house and eat if he didn't buy the food! No man will lay up in my bed if he ain't paying my mortgage! No man will even turn on a damn light in here if he ain't paying the light bill!" *Here she goes again with her speech that I've heard over and over again. Holding the spatula in one hand with the hand on her hip!*

"I'm not a gold digger Mom, I'm not like you!" I sat down at the table knowing what I was in for.

"You're right, you are a fool! This is not gold digging! You didn't get shit out of him, but he sucked the life out of you! Had you lying on a couch with a funky ass, ready to die and the nigga ain't paid one damn bill. Never even brought your son a damn diaper! Your dumb ass can't sleep or eat! You almost lost your job behind his no good ass! Tell me, what sleep is he losing? You can't, because he's not! As long as these men can find dumb ass women like you, they're going to keep on doing what they do!" My mother put down the spatula and sat at the table across from me.

"I was in love, Mom. Maybe you should try it one day and then you will understand where I'm coming from! Don't talk down to me until you've actually gave a damn about a man!" Normally I just keep quiet and suck it up, but not today.

"You think I'm this way for the hell of it! No Chris, a man made me this way! It only took me once to get hurt and I didn't like it! But I'll tell you what; he took care of me! My bills were paid and I didn't go without! This new breed of woman is some kind of a special pathetic! Y'all want to sit around, cry and beg for a man that's not even worthy of one tear! That dog that you laid up with is now another woman's problem. You should be happy and jumping for joy!" She slammed her fist on the table.

"Yes, I should but I'm not! I hear what you're saying, but it doesn't change the fact that he hurt me, and I am human I have feelings!" I snapped back.

"You need to ask yourself, 'What made you think that you were so special?' That dog wasn't hiding anything; he would drive by and beep the horn with another bitch in the car! I call and tell you and you just brush it off your shoulders! As long as he was coming home to you, you felt some kind of entitlement! I have dealt and deal with plenty of men, it just depends on which one of my needs need to be met on that day! Some belong to other women, some don't, but those that do, I could never take seriously because what he does to one woman, he will do to me. I'm not desperate enough to make my mind believe anything different. I'm damn sure not falling in love! You want a no good dog, then go get you another one because there are a lot of them out here barking!"

"If I wanted Poncho, I could still have him. He's been calling my phone and leaving me messages! I'm not dealing with him by my choice! Everything that you are saying, I already know this! I was stupid and played the fool! I'm trying to get myself together for me and my son! This is why I hate talking to you about anything! You're always so negative; you never have anything positive to say! How about you saying, 'Chris, I'm proud of you for sticking to your guns.' How about saying, 'Chris, I know you're hurting but it's going to be okay.' How about you saying, 'Chris, come here, let me give you a hug.' No, all I get is a mother ranting on and on about what I shouldn't have done!" *People can say what they want to say but it doesn't change the fact that my heart is hurting.*

"What you want is for me to give you a pity party and I'm not going to do that! You should have learned from watching me! Your sisters did and I haven't had to dry up too many of their tears! You're always crying and upset about what the same dog that strays did to you on a daily basis. Month after month you come to us for help; help with the bills, and help for the baby, the shit gets played out, Chris! I'm not even mad that the dog got married, I'm happy that he's no longer your burden, but what I'm pissed off about, is the fact that your dumb ass would still be in that mess of a relationship if he didn't get married. It should have been you leaving him a long time ago! The good Lord has a way of opening shut eyes to the blind!"

"I'm so glad that I have Liz to talk to because you make me feel like shit!" I yelled.

"You should feel like shit, that's all you been dealing with is SHIT! That's even more stupid, you talking to Liz, your pretend friend! All of them altercations that the two of you had! Have you forgotten that you two were like *Holy Field* and *Mike Tyson*? Every time I turned around that chick was outside of this house acting a fool! I'm out there breaking up fights, replacing tires and windows! You wouldn't even have her arrested because of that dog! Too scared he was going to leave you if his woman was in jail, where she belonged!"

"We got past all of that and so should you! She is my friend and she helps me out a lot! Liz has been my support system; she calls me to make sure that I'm okay! When I'm having a bad day she's the shoulder that I have to cry on. When I need her to come and get my son or even pick him up from daycare, she does that! If I'm broke and need a few dollars, she's the one that puts money in my pocket! The best part about it, I never have to ask, she just does it! Now that's a friend! You wouldn't know anything about that because you have none! Where are your friends at, Mom?" *Yep, I'm throwing shots; she's coming for me on the wrong damn day!*

"Kudo's to Liz. Tell her I said thank you! Tell her I said take a bow for being the fakest bitch alive! There's no way in hell that girl just all of a sudden forgave you! Don't come crying to me when you wake up, because right now, you're asleep once again! You just keep setting yourself up for disaster!" Mom threw her hands up in the air like she was tired of me.

"You know Mom, y'all have a nice time; I'm out of here!" *I made up in my mind, this would be the last time that woman made me cry.* I grabbed my son, put him in my car and pulled the hell off!

*****

I've never been able to go to my mother for comfort. Whatever happened in her life has her scorned. She's mean and vindictive; my two sister's act just like her. I'm tired of her talking down to me. They just want me to be a ho like them, fucking this one and that one. At least I know who my child's father is. I can't say the same for my sisters, or better yet, for my mother either.

I had so many daddies growing up that my friends were confused and so was I. My mother had me calling Earl, Raymond, Mark, Luis, and Scott, daddy. The good thing was I got showered with a bunch of gifts for birthdays and Christmas. The bad thing was it was hard for me to keep friends. By the time they went home and asked their mother why they only had one daddy and I had five, it was a wrap. My friends could no longer play with me.

My mother thought that shit was funny, but it used to hurt the hell out of me. One day I realized that I was the one that was different, so I started asking questions to all my daddies and all hell broke loose. I guess I blew up Mommy Dearest's spot! Once they realized that she was getting paid five times over, one by one they all disappeared from her trifling ass!

My own family didn't fuck with us, all because of my mother. She couldn't be trusted. Let one of my aunts have more than her and she's the type to go after their man. She would get to flirting and flinching her right eye. She had to be the center of attention. It was always a competition between her and her sisters; the same way she tried it with me and my sisters.

From now on, I'm going to keep my distance. All they do is sit around and talk bad about me. Then she has the nerve to throw back in my face about how she helped me! No more of that, I'm all set on her! If I was starving I wouldn't ask her or my sisters for a piece of bread. It's okay; Christine Willard will be okay! I just have to get over this hump.

CHAPTER 16

THE BUM SQUAD

PONCHO

"Dominique, you're playing games with me!" Rich was screaming in the phone. "I want to see my kids!"

I guess she must have hung up on him. This shit was getting played out. Every day Rich was on the phone arguing with Dominique to see his kids. *I'm not going through all of that. Maybe that's what Chris wants, but I don't have the energy for all of that!*

"What's the deal?" I asked, as I could see the frustration on Rich's face getting worse by the minute.

"Same things, she keeps saying, 'Go see your other kids!' I don't know how much more of this I can take! Dominique wants a divorce, but she has to wait a year for us to be separated. I'm trying to get back in so she can't do it, but in the mean time she's taking me for child support! I stopped over at Rob's house the other day and the sheriff served me with court papers. She knows that I'm not working yet!" Rich said sounding depressed.

"Damn, she ain't playing! Well it doesn't make sense to get a job now because all you're going to be left with is pennies. That's why my baby mamas can forget me ever working. I'm down there for seven of my kids. The only two that didn't bother was Chris and Liz. That's why half of them don't even know where I lay my head at. I'm not going in nobody's courtroom. I keep ducking them sheriffs left and right! You should have run, now you're fucked! If you don't go then you'll have a warrant! These women kill me, trying to hold a child over our heads, like keeping them hostage is going to do something! Be like me, stop calling Dominique and let her ass know that your sperm still works! You can always go make another one! Kids are replaceable; Chris thinks she's doing something when she knows how I get down!"

"Poncho, I have a bond with mine. I miss them; my kids are my world. I can't just leave a part of me running around out here. I want them in my life; kids need their father. I don't want my daughter or son growing up with daddy issues. I want them to always know that they can come to me about and for anything. I want to show them guidance and protection. I'm not leaving mine to hang and dry. Well, not these two anyway. Now the other three, I have to let go of the resentment that I have for Keisha, but in due time I'm going to deal with them!" Rich said, sounding like a hypocrite. *He should hear himself.*

"Okay, have it your way but my way works better…less aggravation. I'm only bothered when I feel like it! That's their fault for thinking that they can hurt me by keeping my kids away from me. What's up with that Keisha situation anyway? Shawty still treating you right after all that mess?"

"DCF has the kids, Keisha is an unfit mother. I have to go to court about that next week, as a matter of fact. They want me to have full custody, but I don't have a place to bring them kids! Mika's cool but you know once you get caught up in a lie with a woman, they never let you live it down. Now she doesn't trust me. I've been laying low and chilling out. I'm trying to get back in her good graces." Rich said walking around a circle. Just like his life, going round and round.

"Man, you better milk the system. When you go to court, let the judge know that you don't have a place or money to take care of the kids. I guarantee you they'll give you a place, a check every month and some food stamps, plus daycare. That will help you with your child support case." I suggested. *Shit, at least he would have a permanent roof over his head with some government assistance.*

"If I do that then I'm kissing my marriage bye bye!" Rich waved his hand.

"Well, I hate to be the bearer of bad news, but you kissed your marriage goodbye the moment Keisha got pregnant. See, if you were just fucking her then you probably could have finagled your way up out of that. The thing with this game is you never risk anything that you're not willing to lose. I knew there was a chance that Chris wouldn't want to be bothered with me, but I was willing to take the gamble. Yes, a part of me thought that she would be over it by now and we could just kick it again like we used to, but I'm not mad at the situation that I put myself in. You have to accept what's done and move on from here. I say if Shawty is making you happy then make a life with her and y'all can raise those kids together. Trying to get Dominique back, man you're just beating a dead horse!" I was trying to give my main man some knowledge.

"You make sense, but I'm going to keep on trying. I just got caught up in the moment. I used to go to Keisha to vent about Dominique when she would be getting on my nerves. She was cool at first; things just started happening. Before I knew it, I was into something that I really didn't want to be in. She would tell me all the time, 'Don't worry Rich, I'm not going to say anything.' Then she gets pregnant with this third baby and that's when I knew she was doing this shit on purpose. I told her, 'Don't get pregnant again or I'm out,' and she did it again." Rich said pissed off.

"That's a lot of moments that you got caught up in, Bro! She heard you complaining and used that to her advantage and you fell for the bait. Keisha was never really your friend, she had motive. These chicks know what they be doing. When she had baby number one you should have ran. You chose to stay and do it again. You can't really blame her! Why the hell you think I have so many baby mamas? If I'm not with you like that, what the hell makes them think that I want a baby with them? I accept my kids because I know I was there, but they get what they get! I never asked for no baby. Just because I stuck my dick in them did not mean that was the go ahead card to go and get pregnant." Some of these women just have to learn the hard way. That's why I treat them accordingly.

"I know, I know! Yeah, it's just fucking with me hard that she won't let me see my kids. I know what I did was wrong but why make the kids suffer? I know they've been asking about me. Mika doesn't have any kids, sometimes I'm looking at her like, 'I hope you don't try and trap me!' Five is more than enough for me. I'm going to sit her down and have a conversation about when and if she wants kids. We both need to be in agreement." Rich said it as if women listen. *Didn't Keisha just stick him with three?*

"You can try it, but I've had plenty of those conversations. Here I am, eleven kids later! The best thing for you to do is strap up; make sure. I would, if I could deal with condoms; I get no satisfaction out of them. I'm better off using my right hand." I laughed.

"I have to try and get my life in order. I can't be hanging out here all day with the fellas anymore. I think I finally hit rock bottom. I went to the gas station and put three dollars in the tank. Now you know that's sad." Rich was looking pitiful as hell. *I almost feel bad for him.*

"Here man, take this twenty and go get you some gas! I got you; keep your head up. What's up with Shawty, she ain't holding you down?" *Inquiring minds want to know because if you can't get no dollars, then why is he even with her?*

"Thanks man, I needed this. You know I'm still in the dog-house, so I haven't been asking her for anything." Rich said, putting that twenty in his pocket.

"That's why you need a little side piece to pick up the slack." I used to like being in the dog-house, it gave me more time with my side chicks. I wasn't losing any sleep.

"Naw Poncho, that's what got me in this mess in the first place. Sometimes them side pieces can be more of a headache than the main chick! I'm good!" Rich sounded as if he was exhausted from women.

*****

"Damn man, sorry I'm late. The UI Company came and turned off the lights again. Tisha got her priorities all fucked up. She went and got a whole weave put in yesterday, nails and toes done, but didn't pay the damn light bill! I had to get the food out the fridge and freezer to store it at Dominique's once again!" Quan just rolls up on me and Rich with the same shit, different month. Tisha never pays the damn bills until something gets cut off. *He should have been expecting it.* "I'm tired of this shit, I'm about to be like Mickey and Trey; get me a bitch in the projects with everything included. This doesn't make any sense. "

Rich and I needed this laugh after coming off a serious conversation.

"Yall laughing, this is not any funny business! I have to find me somewhere to crash until she gets some damn electricity. Y'all know a nigga likes to see!" Only my man Quan would come out his mouth sideways. Tisha has kids, he ain't worried about them seeing, only him. *If they call me selfish what do you call him?*

"Man you know you go through this every other month." I had to remind Quan.

"Yo man, have you seen my kids?" Rich asked, changing the conversation.

"Yeah, they're straight! I can tell they miss you though! Every time they see me they're asking for you. I was telling Dominique she needs to let you see them kids, regardless of how she feels about you! Hopefully she will budge pretty soon!" Quan put his hand on Rich's shoulder. "The squad knows that it's bothering you and we're here for you man."

"Thanks man, I appreciate it! Make sure you tell my kids that I love them and daddy will see them soon!" Rich said.

"Yep, I got you!" Quan replied.

*****

We went into quiet mode just looking at the cars riding up and down the street while Rich's eyes was filling up with tears, mumbling to himself about God knows what. *I know it's time for me to bounce; nigga can't be embarrassing me like this on the Ave. If he needs to shed some tears, go home and do that shit!*

I'm so glad I can't make out what he's saying. He can make babies, do his dirt and expect no consequences. *It doesn't work like that main man.* I keep trying to tell these fools that I grew up with a bunch of women, so I know how a woman thinks, for the most part. Dominique is fed up. Just like when Liz was done with me, she was done. I like exploring new pussy so you'll never catch me crying over one.

CHAPTER 17

MEET & GREET

LIZ

My relationship with Tyson was starting to get serious. We both decided to be committed to one another. I spent time at his place, but most of the time he was over here with me, along with his son.

My girls and his son seemed to get along just fine, other than a little bickering here and there, which that's what kids do. Other than that, we weren't having any problems.

Tyson and I were still in our honeymoon stage. He was getting to know my ways and I was getting to know his. So far, we were a match made in heaven.

*****

I just received a promotion on my job. I have now moved up to Supervisor. I don't get to see Mika as much; I'm in my own private office, in and out of meetings most days. The most I see her is in passing, which makes her hate the job even more.

She's been looking for another job. I kind of figured that when I took the position, because the only reason she stayed so long was because of our friendship.

We both enjoyed working with one another, but when my boss approached me about the position, I thought about how much better me and the girls would be off. I got a hefty raise. I just couldn't let that opportunity slip on by me.

I thought today would be a great day to have Mika and Chris over for some girl chat and just to catch up. I see and talk to Chris more than I do with Mika, because of the kids mainly. We're still looking out for each other and growing closer every day. My once enemy is more like a sister to me.

If Poncho could see us now he would probably pass out. Now I know what the Bible means when it says, 'What the devil meant for bad, God will turn it around for the good.'

Chris has been so helpful to me. I wish all women would just come together and help one another out.

*****

"Hey ladies, Chris this is Mika. Mika this is Chris. You two finally get to meet." They both exchanged welcoming 'Hellos' as they sat across from each other at the kitchen table. They always heard about one another, but today is their first time actually meeting.

"What you got over here cooking?" Chris was peeping in the pan.

"I'm just deep frying some chicken. I'm going to make us a salad and the kids some fries." I said grinning from ear to ear. It felt good to have some downtime. Don't get me wrong, I love me some Tyson, but I love spending time with my girls too.

*****

"So Chris, not only do you know Rich, but you know Keisha too, right?" Mika asked.

"Yeah, Keisha and I used to be real cool back in the day. We met at Cross and I just clicked with her crazy ass. She was always suspended for fighting somebody. The school got tired and expelled her so we lost contact, but then last year, at the Freddie Fixer Parade, I ran into her, so we rekindled our friendship. We got into an argument, so I haven't spoken to her. I was thinking about reaching out since they took her kids, but I decided against the negativity. I just wish her well from a distance."

"Yo, she is really crazy! You don't even look like the type that would hang with her! I'm not trying to offend you or anything, but that chick is off her rocker! I'm glad they took them babies from her. All she was worried about was me and Rich! I guess she just said, 'Forget the babies!' She had her newborn baby in that stroller screaming from the top of her lungs. The other two stair steps were out there screaming, 'Daddy.' It was a mess!" Mika shook her head.

"Well I can say that she did take care of her kids and she loves them. Keisha has always been a little off, but when it comes down to Rich, she goes into another ram of crazy! I was through with her when she had the nerve to call Dominique and tell her everything. Now how ratchet is that?"

"Oh wow!" Mika said with her mouth wide open. "So she called his wife, three babies later. I can't see what he saw in her. Why not just be with his wife? You know me, Liz." Mika looked over at me. "I was asking Rich a lot of questions. He lied to me about everything. I don't trust him."

"You shouldn't, if he would sleep with his wife's cousin, then I feel sorry for what he would do to you. I'm telling you Mika, leave that situation alone. He's been cheating on Dominique even before Keisha. I remember the days when Dominique and I would be catching him and Poncho out there. I know you like him, but he's just another fuck up that will never change!" I said, trying to convince Mika to let go now. *Rich will manipulate the hell out of her if she doesn't. He had a wonderful trainer.*

"I've been seriously considering it. I don't let him take my car anymore. Most of the time Poncho pulls up and beeps the horn for him to come out. I stopped giving him money, it's not like he's paying any bills. We were alright up until that incident. Then not only was he hiding kids, but a wife too. I didn't find out about a wife until I was talking to you, Liz, and you let that out of the bag.

When I approached him about a wife then he came clean, but if you had never told me then I still wouldn't know. He would have had another hidden secret. I'm starting to feel like a used up fool! Rich comes across as this great guy that has it all together, but he's nothing but a good ass liar." Mika said sounding fed up.

"They all do, that's how that crew rolls! I'm with Liz, get out now before you have all of them in your apartment eating up your food, chilling, and making you feel like you're the coolest home girl in the world. Then one day you wake up, only to find out that they were all in a wedding you knew nothing about. I have nothing to say to none of them niggas. I would like to spit on each and every one of them though! They're all a bunch of sorry ass losers! Cut your losses, spare your feelings, and guard your heart!" Chris chimed in.

Oh Lord, Chris was getting in her feelings again. I want to catch up, not spend my day man bashing. "Okay, let's change the subject." I suggested.

"So how's it going between you and Tyson?" Mika asked.

Whenever I hear his name a smile comes over my face. "It's going pretty good, I can't complain." I noticed Chris was sitting at the table rolling her eyes. *Now I'm starting to sense a bit of bitterness coming from her.* I'm trying to be understanding. I know the last thing she wants to hear is about how good my relationship is going, when she's still hurting from the one she was in. When I talk to her about Tyson, I keep it real short and give her one word answers.

"Good, that's it? I want to know more, like some details or something! What's all the secrecy about?" Mika asked.

Mika knows me well, so I gave her the, 'shut the fuck up' look and glanced over at Chris. *I hope that she can read between the lines, that now is not the time.* "There's really not much to say, I don't want to jinx anything. So far I'm happy as can be, he's special to me." I said, hoping that would be enough.

"I'm happy for you, Liz. I think Tyson is the one for you. As long as he's putting a smile on your face then that's all that matters to me. It took a long time for you to let someone in, so he must be someone special. I saw you turn your nose up at the thought of a man. This is a huge leap for you." Mika said sincerely.

"I hope it stays that way. I don't trust no man. To me, it's all a front. Once they get what they want, then they start treating you like shit and 'bye bye;' it is on to the next! Let me tell you, Mika, how good Poncho was...he had me thinking that I was the only one and I knew he was with Liz. I used to say there's no way he's sleeping with her, not the way he is with me. In my mind I had this vision of them two being more like roommates and it had nothing to do with what he said. It was all in the way that man treated me. He was such a gentleman, massaging my feet, licking my toes, making me dinner, lighting candles, running bath water; when I tell you that this man is gifted, believe me. He never has to spend one dime on a chick, but by the time he's done with putting on his charm, you feel like he just spent a million dollars on you! Chicks would be saying that they was with him this day, that day, girl I wouldn't believe them! I thought they were lying on him, but now that I know what I know, he really was with them. He'll make love to me in the morning, run over to Monica, hit her off, and then come back home and make love to me again. He had me fooled. That day when Liz put him out and he was standing at my door with his stuff, girl I thought I won the lottery. I was so happy!" Chris was rehashing her reasoning for being with Poncho.

"I'm sorry that he did that to you and Liz, but all men aren't the same. I believe in giving a man a fair chance, you just never know. Liz calls me gullible because I trust too easy. I've been hurt a lot in the past, but I refuse to get bitter. I like feeling butterflies all the way down to the pit of my stomach. Love makes this world go around and there is no greater feeling. You can find you a man with the same qualities as Poncho, with a job, that will take care of you and your son. Holding on to pain will always leave a sour taste in your mouth and you'll never be open to feel again." Mika was pouring her heart out.

*****

I was just finishing up the food, preparing plates and listening. *Mika was talking some real knowledge.* "Like I told you before Chris, it takes time."

Chris turned her nose up at my statement. "Yeah, yeah, that's what they say! I know one thing; I'm getting my appetite back because I'm hungry. Just give me my plate, please!" Chris reached her hand out.

"It's coming," I laughed. I laid a blanket on the living room floor for the kids to eat on, since they wanted to eat picnic style. Then I put our plates on the table so we could grub. We must have all been hungry because we all ate in silence.

*****

"Okay ladies, I'm nice and full! Are we ready for some Moscato? I have three bottles of the sweet!" I grabbed the wine glasses and filled them up to the top.

"Oh yes, we are!" Chris and Mika said at the same time.

"I have *Sorry*, *Monopoly*, or *Uno*, which game are we playing tonight?" *It didn't matter to me; the majority will rule.*

"Oh my God, let's play all three. I haven't played these games since I was a kid!" Mika said all excited.

Chris and I were cracking up laughing at Mika. The big kid was coming out in her.

I was a little iffy on how this meet and greet would go, but I'm very pleased that the three of us could sit down, have some girl talk with three different perspectives and agree to disagree. Either way, I think we all learned something and were able to take something from the conversation and apply it to our own lives. Now that I know we can bond like this, we're going to do this more often. I feel like it's good therapy for all three of us.

CHAPTER 18

KEISHA

The judge continued my case again. I was planning on wrapping this thing up, but the prosecutor was trying to give me time in jail, and my public defender was arguing the fact that I have a mental condition. She's trying to say that I suffer from bipolarism and depression that has never been treated. I have to go to see all these doctors for evaluation. I tried to tell Attorney Grey that this is not going to help my DCF case. With all of this going on, I may not ever be considered stable enough to get custody of my children back. Right now I'm getting supervised visitation once a week for an hour. Shit is pissing me off.

I miss Rich so much, and my only connection to him is those kids. I did get a quick glance at him in court; he left out so fast that I couldn't catch him. My stomach was in knots when I saw him with the lame.

Even though he and his bitch are making these charges stick, I still know, that deep down inside, he wants to be with me. Right now he's just trying to impress her.

Both of them have restraining orders against me. All I need is an alibi for what I'm about to do next. I know where the bitch works and if she thinks she's going to be prancing around New Haven with my man, then she better think again. *Young, simple bitch.* I put up with Dominique for years, ain't no way I'm dealing with another one. *How the hell is she going to come out the blue and take what belongs to me?*

That's what's wrong with these stank ass females, they don't know their lane! I warned her the first time when I went over there; she saw what I'm capable of. That's my baby daddy that she's over there playing in the sheets with. I don't have a dime to my name because of all of this mess. Social Services stopped my check, my food stamps got cut off, and now I have a meeting at Section 8. I need my kids back in order for me to survive. *How the hell do they expect me to eat?*

*****

Since Rich is the cause of all of this, I have made up my mind that today he will see me! I've decided to do a stake out, outside this bitch's apartment. *I'm not going anywhere; he must be in there.*

I know she went back to work after court because I saw her car parked during my stroll to the bus stop. I wanted to bust out her windows and flatten her tires, but there were too many people around.

Because she lives in a secure building, I have to wait for somebody to come out before I can get in. I'm trying to catch Rich by surprise. I know his weaknesses. If this plan doesn't work, then I'm back to Plan A…fucking her up!

*****

Lucky me, this lady is coming out. *Come on lady hurry your slow ass up!*

As soon as she opened the door, I walked in. Looking around I saw the exit sign. I opened the door and made my way up to the second floor and walked straight to her apartment.

I knocked on the door a couple times, no answer. *He must have went back to sleep, but he's going to wake up.* I'm trying not to bang too hard. I don't want the lames' neighbors to start looking out. I can hear him coming; my stomach is in knots again.

Rich opened the door and tried to close it, but I barged in and shut the door behind me. *He will deal with me today!* He might be a man, but when I'm mad I have the strength of a gorilla.

*****

"Get out, Keisha! Why are you here anyway?" Rich said very nastily.

I should go upside his head but my heart is melting from looking at him. "I need you, that's why I'm here!" *I said what I wasn't supposed to say; ugh this damn heart of mind is not matching up with my mind.*

"You don't need me, you fucked shit up! You must want to go back to jail!" Rich yelled.

"I just want to talk to you. I had to come over here. You have me on your blocked list and when I try to call from any other numbers, you won't answer. How can I fix us*?" Damn it, a tear came rolling out.*

"There is no 'us,' Keisha! You told Dominique everything; I wanted to be the one to tell her when the time was right." *Rich is full of it, he would have never told her. Right now I have to play this his way.*

"I'm sorry. I got mad. I can take it back; I'll call her up and tell her that the kids don't belong to you! I'll make her think that I was lying and then we can go back to the way it used to be between us. I didn't even show up at court; I'm not cooperating with the prosecutor!" *Now I had his full attention.* Rich's whole expression changed and his eyes lit up.

"How can you make her believe you? I already kind of admitted to being with you. I told her I was drunk, which I was! Then you would have to come up with a baby daddy. It's not going to work." Rich was shaking his head but talking to me in a much softer tone.

"It's not going to hurt to try. We can work together and even get our kids back! All we have to do is make sure that our stories line up! You have to convince your lame to drop my charges!" I said looking around her apartment, wanting to tear shit up.

"She will never agree to drop the charges, plus the state will pick them right back up! But back to Dominique, she barely answers my calls and I just got to see the kids the other day. She dropped them off at her mother's. She doesn't want to be anywhere near me." *Aww, Rich looked so sad. This is what I'm talking about; he's more worried about those kids than our kids. He better get that bitch to drop those charges.*

"Don't worry about Dominique; I know how to get to her. Have you forgotten that we are family, whether we want to be or not? I still owe her an ass whooping, but if she puts her hands on me then I will go in defense mode. She's lucky nothing happened to me or the baby. She was trying to kill me, Rich!" I had to emphasize to Rich about what Dominique did and how nice I'm being, considering all that she did. *This should count for something.*

"Well Keisha, what did you think was going to happen? You know how she is; I know damn well that you didn't expect anything different. Let's just take it one step at a time and see what we can come up with. I'm happy that you came to your senses. If this should work out, don't try and cross me again! I want my name cleared, and I'll work on Mika to see what we can come up with!" Rich ran his fingers through his hair; he usually does that when he's relieved. *Now he's in a much better mood than when I first barged in.*

"Now come here, Daddy." I walked over and grabbed him by his pants. "Don't you miss what I can do for you? I know this lame can't put it down like I can! I miss you Rich, I just love you so much!" I bent down on my knees, unzipping his pants, while rubbing my nuts that were out on loan to this lame for far too long.

"Keisha, stop it. You know I haven't touched you since I saw that baby bump! Uh, don't do that! Keisha, please!" Rich uttered with a moan of pleasure. *I knew he missed me.*

"I want you to say, 'Keisha, please suck my dick!' Nobody sucks it like me, isn't that what you used to tell me? Does she suck it better than me? Does she? Answer me baby!" I asked in-between slobs. *I just want my cum in my mouth again. This dick belongs to me and he better realize it.*

"Uh no, nobody sucks it like you! Uh, my cum snatcher!" Rich put his hands on my head and started pushing me in deeper, just like I like it.

I was too busy sucking my dick. I heard the door unlock. I figured it was that lame about to come in, but I wasn't stopping. *Maybe she could learn a thing or two. She should have stayed her ass at work. Just watch bitch!*

CHAPTER 19

THE BUM SQUAD

PONCHO

$\mathcal{C}$hurch service was off the hook. We had a guest Pastor and all them women...beautiful women just flowing in there. It got so good to them that almost the whole congregation was shouting. That's my favorite part, when the dresses and skirts get to flying in the air; I get to watch all them asses bouncing up and down. Whoever this Pastor was, he needs to come back more often.

Good thing wifey was on Usher duty today because I couldn't control my eyes and my manhood was standing at attention. I kept sticking my hand down there while covering my lap with the Bible. My balls were full and ready to explode.

I keep trying to tell the squad that they need to roll with me on a Sunday. Church is where it's at, not a club, not these streets. There are plenty of women that you don't even know existed up in here. Even after service was over I had to sit for an extra fifteen minutes trying to calm myself down. Normally, I try to be the first one running out because I usually sit in the back. With wifey ushering today, she put me in the middle; won't happen again. Plus, I like the back. I get a full view of all the ladies.

Next Sunday I'm making the squad go with me so they can see firsthand what I'm talking about. I can almost guarantee that they won't miss a Sunday. I can see us now...all meeting up together, that's what's up. Yep, me and my whole squad.

Wifey knows my usual routine; we drive separate because she has to be here extra early. After church I go and hang out at the flea market for a while, grab a bite to eat, and chill outside the car, flexing in my suit. I like for the people to see me in a different light. *Yeah, I know how to clean up well.* Wifey goes home to cook us some Sunday dinner and calls me when it's ready, that's when I head back to the house.

*****

Today I'm going to stop by Liz's house to check on my girls. I haven't seen them in months. I heard Liz has a Boo that she's head over heels for. I need to congratulate her, make my presence known, so my girls don't think that daddy just disappeared out of their lives. I'm going to let them know that I will be getting them some weekends just like me and Chris used to do. Ain't nothing changed but the woman. *I hope they're home.* I'm on some pop up shit, just in case Liz is in one of her moods where she feels like arguing about what I don't do. I'm not in the mood to hear it, and my girls will block all of that. Liz won't argue with me in front of them. She claims we did that enough when we were together. She wants the girls to see us healthy parenting.

*****

When I pulled up I saw Chris's car outside and immediately changed my mind. I heard they were buddies now, I have to chuckle at that thought. Guess it's true, I'm seeing for myself. *I won't get caught up in that crossfire.* I have to deal with them one at a time. I know Liz won't act out, but Chris will.

*****

Guess I'll go ahead and head home early. Maybe wifey is in the mood to make love to me in-between her cooking. She ain't been on top of her game. I need to let her know that her husband has a hell of a sexual appetite. When my dick gets hard I need to be satisfied.

Honesty has been seeing me a whole lot more than usual. Wifey be having headaches and tired from work. No wonder these career women are always being cheated on and stay single. They don't know how to multitask.

Pleasing your man should always come first; everything else should be secondary. I realize she's practically running a corporation, but she has to remember that she has a household to run too. I don't like being neglected, and it's something I'm not used to.

She thinks she can tickle my fancy with gifts and clothes, but I love pussy.

Don't get me wrong, my lifestyle is fine and dandy but it don't mean shit to me if I ain't getting no ass. It's only been a couple of months; marriage is new to the both of us, so I've been remaining humble. I'm in need for her to get her freak on. It's bad enough when she gets her period, she doesn't want to be touched. She acts like a towel and bath can't help that; always going by what that Bible says. I like to fuck three hundred and sixty five days a year. Straight like that, and if she's going to go by the good book then she should know that pleasing me is her first priority, besides God himself. Don't be half ass with it; be all the way in! Yes, it's time to have that talk today!

*****

I walk in the house, smelling the aroma from the food. *Damn it smells good. If only she sexed me as good as this food, I might be home more often.* I peeped in the pots. She got some collard greens going, macaroni boiling for baked mac and cheese, ham in the oven, potatoes in a bowl for some potato salad, cornbread already mixed up. *Yeah, I'm about to eat good for dinner tonight.* I'm smiling from ear to ear.

Wifey has the music playing, and to my surprise, it isn't gospel for a change. *Oh yeah, I hear Silk!* "Freak me baby, let me lick you up and down." I'm singing along. I go upstairs, and crack open the door to our room. *Yes, this is how I like to see my women. No need for that talk.*

She's in a black negligee with some silk black stilettoes. *The good Lord must have been talking to her.* I'm just admiring the view until I see Honesty come from out our bathroom, butt ass naked!

"What the fuck is going on here?"

CHAPTER 20

LIZ

$\mathcal{T}$oday was moving day for me. Tyson and I decided that it didn't make sense for him to be paying a mortgage and me paying full rent. We practically live together anyway. It made more sense to do it this way. Why not save some money since our relationship was at the next level. His idea, but I was damn sure thinking it.

For now we will stay at his house, then eventually venture out and buy a house together. I explained to him that I wasn't comfortable with buying property unless we were married. Tyson agreed with me and said he wouldn't have it any other way. I'm just glad that we are on the same page.

*****

We threw a small cookout in his back yard, just to see how our families gelled. Our mothers seemed to get along just fine. Matter of fact, they had a lot in common and planned to go shopping together. It was like one big family and we both couldn't be happier. I feel like we are a match made in heaven. *God had to send this man to me! I'm so grateful to Mika for convincing me to go out with her.*

*****

My girls are happy. Tyson is like that father figure that they never had. Poncho has always been in and out, never showing any stability, but Tyson has been there. Helping them with their homework, taking them out for playdates and giving me some 'me time.'

The girls haven't even asked about Poncho lately, and that's fine with me. *I hope he stays away they don't need that confusion in their lives.* One of these days, I'm going to call Poncho's other seven baby mamas to see if we can get all the kids together. Maybe meet at the park so they can all be introduced as brothers and sisters.

*****

As we were moving out, Chris was moving in. She needed a new start, especially since she was up for eviction. It's hard to catch up on bills once you're behind. I was happy to hand over my place to her; my lease wasn't up anyway. I probably could have talked to my landlord and got him to let me out the lease, but I wanted to help Chris out.

I told Chris that if she ever runs short that I got her, and I meant it. Tyson put me in a position where I can save even more money. A win-win for the both of us. She had more than enough space.

The only problem was that I needed to contact Poncho and let him know that I moved. *I'll text him a little later. Don't need him popping up and finding Chris.* She was finally detoxing from Poncho, now when she talked about him the tears weren't flowing, just anger. Her priorities were in order; she was all about her son.

Chris was depending on me more, and staying away from her corrupt family. Fine with me, she needs some positivity in her life. From what she told me, her family is trifling. Her mother looks so innocent; but she's not. I can believe that she's as mean as Chris says she is, back in the day when Chris and I would go at it. She always involved herself. I could see the pain in her eyes as she tells me stories about her growing up. A mother should always try to build her kids up and raise them to respect themselves, not the opposite…especially girls. I'm raising three girls, just like Chris's mother, and I would never raise mine to fuck for money. *Shame on that woman for getting mad at Chris because she chose not to be a ho!*

*****

While I have the girls unpacking their rooms I need to make a quick run back to the apartment and grab the rest of the miscellaneous stuff that I left.

162

I gave Tyson a kiss and told him that I would be right back. When I got back to the apartment, Chris was busy unpacking her stuff.

*****

"Hey girl, I'm just here to grab the last of my things." I said.

"Yeah, don't you think this was kind of quick you moving in with him so soon. It hasn't even been six months yet?" Chris asked with an attitude. *I think she wants me all to herself or something. This is ridiculous. She always has something negative to say, but then again, I have to remember where she came from.*

"Well, the way our relationship is going and the fact that we're making plans for our future, what difference does it make if it's one year from now or one month? If we feel like it's meant to be, then it's nobody else's business but ours!" I snapped back at Chris.

"I'm just saying…you're putting a whole lot of trust into that man. What if things go sour, then what's your plan? I have to make sure that my son and I are secure over here." Chris asked. *Now it makes a little bit of sense. She's worried about me having to move back.*

"I don't have any other plan, this has to work! I wouldn't have made a move like this if I didn't trust Tyson! That would just be stupid on my part! In the event that it does go sour, we can always move back in here with you!" I said jokingly.

"Of course, just as long as you don't put me out! Are you thinking about marrying him or just shacking up?" I sensed that Chris was throwing a little bit of shade with this question.

"Yes, we're talking about it. Sometime next year I will become his wife and I can't wait to say I do! We're going to do something small, just close family and friends. We both want our wedding to be very intimate." *Little does she know, I've already been browsing around for dresses.*

"Oh my God, are you serious? I at least thought that y'all would live together for a while before going overboard! Now you're really living in fantasy land!" Chris said with her eyes popping out her head and mouth wide open.

"This is not a fantasy, at all! This is so real for me and Tyson! Now you're acting like a straight up bitch. I don't know what your problem is, but you never have anything nice to say when it comes down to me and him! I'm getting real sick and tired of your shit!" *Chris pissed me off now. I've been waiting to have somebody that loves me and only has eyes for me, all my damn life. She won't be in my wedding if she keeps acting like this.*

"Sorry if I'm not jumping for joy, but Tyson ain't no better than the rest of these no good ass men running around New Haven! You keep putting him on this pedestal like he doesn't have a dick!" Chris stopped to glance at her phone that was ringing back to back.

"Maybe you should answer that! I'm leaving before we end up arguing. I'm in a good mood, and I want to keep it that way! When you get over your misery, give me a call!" I walked out.

I was so mad that I forgot my box that I packed up sitting on the table. *Now I have to go back in there.*

I heard Chris in the bathroom. *Good, now I can grab my box and get the hell out of here without her knowing.* Her phone was still ringing so I peeped over to see who's calling and it was Tyson.

Why in the hell would Tyson be calling Chris, and how in the hell did she have his number? My heart dropped as the tears rolled down my face!

Other Books by Stacey Fenner

A TOXIC LOVE AFFAIR
Available at: Amazon

Tyrone and Daniel are two best friends but total opposites. Tyrone has his woman at home taking care of the kids while he's out playing in the streets. He soon finds out that being too comfortable and secure will cost him everything when he comes home to an empty home.

Will his womanizing ways wreck his life or can he get it together before it's to late?

Daniel on the other hand, is still trying to heal from a messy divorce with Candace five years later. He's tried dating but finds it hard to move on.

Find out what happens with a good-looking man who has money to buy everything but is unfulfilled on the inside. A Toxic Love Affiar is filled with love, lust, hate and drama.

*****

A TOXIC LOVE AFFAIR 2
Available at: Amazon

They say once a good girl is gone she's gone forever, and if you thought Part 1 threw you for a loop, then get ready to do figure 8's this go around.

Belinda sets out on a mission to destroy all her childhood, so-called, friends that have betrayed her. She has no boundaries or limits to her destruction. She has intentions on making each and every one of them pay, and has masterminded a plan that will eventually cause her to self-destruct in the worst way!

Being disloyal to Belinda will cost them everything. Everybody likes to play but nobody wants to pay!

Meanwhile, Daniel finally opens himself up to love again after going through his messy divorce with his scandalous ex-wife, Candace. That won't last too long when a jealous Candace gets wind of the relationship; she throws a monkey wrench trying to exhaust him of all hope. Meanwhile, Daniel is stuck cleaning up the mess Tyrone created.

Find out if Tyrone and Daniel's friendship can survive the aftermath when Daniel gets wind to what Belinda is up to and he feels responsible for her trifling ways. Shocked is an understatement as to how he feels about a woman he once had so much respect for.

*****

A TOXIC LOVE AFFAIR 3
Available at: Amazon

These toxic relationships will take it to another level of trifling in this final installment of the Toxic Love Series.

Tyrone takes a trip back down memory lane and reunites with his drug-addicted mother on a quest to find out who his father is. After hooking up with Dana, Daniel's sister, Tyrone decides to turn in his player card and be a father to all of the children that he has fathered, but karma has a funny way of landing right back in his lap. Getting what he gave in life; will trouble from the past overcome him?

Daniel relocates back to Atlanta to be with Shaunda, the woman that he plans on spending the rest of his life with, but an unexpected visitor will come along and be the interruption of everything. Meanwhile, Shaunda reveals another side of herself that has Daniel questioning her pure existence. As Daniel's hatred toward his ex-best friend, Mr. Tyrone himself, grows after he learns of the secret relationship of Tyrone and Dana.

Sheree and Calvin's marriage is on the rocks once again because of Sheree's obsession in finding Belinda to seek revenge. Sheree bites off more than she can handle when another secret of hers is revealed.

Belinda makes her way back to the states and right back into the arms of her protector, Troy. But of course not without a twist to her madness.

Rivals will come face to face when a funeral places everyone in the same location...but who will meet their untimely demise?

*****

THE COMMANDMENTS OF A FEMALE HUSTLER

Available at: Amazon

Meet the well-known trio, Lala, Binky and Jay, who been rocking and rolling together since their childhood days. Raised in the projects these three had only one thing on their minds, the come up! These ladies will show you how to use what you got to get what you want!

What starts out as 'may the best woman win' ends in a rage of jealousy, dividing the three. After such a betrayal, can their relationship be fixed? What happens when the commandments are no longer followed? One will find love, one will end up behind bars, and one's mind is sick and twisted!

Swift, Jock, and Moose have the east side of Baltimore locked down with the drug game, but stuff gets twisted when there's a murder involved. When relationships fail, sex, lies and love take over. Their loyalty towards one another will be tested in the worst way. Rivals will meet, love will be found and hearts will be changed as the hustler game is taken to a whole new level of disrespect!

Who will be the sell out?

About Stacey Fenner

Instagram: authorstaceyfenner
Twitter: sfenner1
Facebook: www.facebook.com/authorstaceyfenner

You can contact Stacey Fenner at
authorstaceyfenner@gmail.com

Stacey Fenner, was born December 1 and raised in New Haven, CT., the youngest of three. In 1999 Stacey relocated to Atlanta, GA where she resided for a year before moving to Baltimore, MD to care for her parents with her two daughters.

Writing since she was a child was a way to express herself, allowing her to overcome many trials and tribulations. However, she never pursued her gift until 2008. Although she obtained her degree in accounting, and currently works in that field, her passion is and always has been writing.

Stacey's writing career is focused upon novels about relationships. Her first book, A Toxic Love Affair, which was published in April of 2015, landed her in the #37 spot on the Woman's Urban Best Selling list. Her follow-up novel, A Toxic Love Affair Part 2, landed in the # 24 spot on that very same list. Having just recently finished up Part 3 of that series, Stacey is taking the Indie world by storm.

Made in the USA
San Bernardino, CA
10 March 2018